A Place in the Sun

A Place in the Sun

Liberation Theology in the Third World

Theo Witvliet

ORBIS BOOKS
Maryknoll, New York 10545

The Catholic Foreign Mission Society of America (Maryknoll) recruits and trains people for overseas missionary service. Through Orbis Books Maryknoll aims to foster the international dialogue that is essential to mission. The books published however, reflect the opinions of their authors and are not meant to represent the official position of the society.

Translated by John Bowden from the Dutch
Een Plaats onder de Zon. Bevrijdingstheologie in de derde wereld,
published by Uitgeverij Ten Have 1984

First published 1985 by SCM Press Ltd
26-30 Tottenham Road, London N1
and by Orbis Books, Maryknoll, NY 10545

Typeset by Input Typesetting Ltd
and printed in Great Britain by
Richard Clay Ltd (The Chaucer Press),
Bungay, Suffolk

Library of Congress Cataloging in Publication Data

Witvliet, Theo.
  A place in the sun.

  Translation of: Een plaats onder de zon.
  Bibliography: p.
  Includes index.
  1. Liberation theology. 2. Black theology.
3. Ras Tafari movement. 4. Theology, Doctrinal—
Developing countries. I. Title.
BT83.57.W5713 1985   230   84–27229
ISBN 0–88344–404–6 (pbk.)

48,338

Contents

Preface

Liberation theology is usually associated with the Third World, and especially with Latin America. That can lead to misunderstandings. By no means all the theology which nowadays sees the light in the Third World is liberation theology, and by no means all liberation theology is produced in the Third World.

However, the investigation of the various forms of liberation theology presented in this book is limited to Asia, Africa, Latin America and the Caribbean. It does not deal with aspects of liberation theology in the North Atlantic world, where feminist theology is particularly dominant. I have made an exception for black theology in the United States, both because it comes from Africa and because of the prominent place occupied by its representatives in the Ecumenical Association of Third World Theologians (referred to elsewhere in the book as EATWOT).

I can defend this limitation to the Third World only on the basis of practical considerations. The connection between the words 'theology' and 'liberation' has had so many repercussions in the last fifteen years that it is now impossible even to survey all the literature, let alone assimilate it. Even if we limit ourselves to the so-called 'Third World' (which is in fact two-thirds of the world), we plunge into a hazardous, though extremely exciting, adventure. The reason why I have ventured on such an undertaking, leaving aside the fact that I am probably inclined to overestimate my capabilites, is that I am convinced that a survey of the very different forms of liberation theology in other continents is an excellent way for us indirectly to come to terms with the fact that our own theological activity is determined by the society in which we live – and I see the discovery of this fact as a precondition of our arriving at liberating, living forms of theology in our own situation.

And that already says something about the purpose of this book. This is no uncommitted tour of Third-World theology. On the other hand, I am very cautious about taking over what has been discovered elsewhere. Liberation theology, whether in Latin

America or anywhere else, is not an export product on the theological world market, for consumption by anyone who can afford the luxury.

Anyone who allows Third-World theologians a word must also allow them to speak out. And that can be painful for us. Of course they live and work in situations which are not ours. But at the same time we are bound up with these situations through historical, economic, political, cultural and economic ties. Moreover, in the last resort, both we and they are dealing with one and the same messianic reality, which became flesh in this one man, Jesus of Nazareth.

This state of affairs introduces a degree of tension into the encounter with liberation theology in other continents: we are not just confronted with people in other situations but, through them, with ourselves, with our own social commitment. We are asked about our own involvement in the struggle over issues of class, race and sex that is going on in our society.

This tension is directly connected with the tension between the particular and the universal which is characteristic of liberation theology. Any theology of liberation which does justice to the by no means insignificant claims inherent in its very name takes its point of departure in the specific features of a particular situation of oppression and dependence, but *that is not the whole story*. It has a universal dimension, not despite but *in* the specific character of its commitment to the rejected of the earth, and this does justice both to the inclusiveness of the biblical narrative and to the judgment inherent in that narrative. We are concerned with this universal dimension, but... it is only accessible to those who take the trouble to grasp the particularity seriously and put up with it – and in this case that means putting up with the strangeness and the otherness of this theology. As in all good theology, so here too the way which leads to knowledge runs from the specific to the universal, and not vice versa.

So we must not allow ourselves to be infatuated by the question 'What must we do here and now?', a question which is asked so often and which can be so troublesome. Raising this discussion question is often a disguised attempt at evading the challenge posed by a confrontation with liberation theology in other contexts. Anyone who really accepts what Gustavo Gutiérrez, James Cone and all the others have to say will find soon enough that, put in this way, the question can never lead to a fruitful answer.

I am not sorry that the space at my disposal does not allow me to discuss this and similar questions in detail. It is difficult enough to do justice to the questions and problems with which people are wrestling in Asia, Africa and Latin America. This is no more than a guidebook, something which comes midway between a survey and an interpretation. I am not aiming at any kind of completeness. I could only hint at a number of important matters in a sentence or two. So this book is also a reference book: if you feel an irresistible urge to pick up and study books by those who are mentioned here, the writing of my own book will have been well worth while.

Because people other than professional theologians are interested in liberation theology, where possible I have tried to avoid difficult technical jargon. And there are no footnotes. However, at the end of the book there is a bibliography which gives a selection of books on the questions discussed.

At a later date, Deleuze and Guattari said of their book *L'Anti-Oedipe*: 'We wrote the Anti-Oedipus between us. Because each of us is made up of several people, it turned out to be a real mixture.' I could not get this remark out of my mind while I was working on *A Place in the Sun*. It is certainly an illusion to suppose that one writes a book all by oneself, in the first person singular. So in the following pages I have avoided the word 'I'. The writing of a book like this is a process in which many people have shared. Some of them are mentioned by first name and surname in quotations and references, but most of them remain anonymous. I cannot fail to mention here the many first-year students of the Theological Faculty of the University of Amsterdam in which I work. Their questions and comments on the syllabus from which this book has emerged have influenced its final form and content. An important contribution was also made by those who were prepared to go through the manuscript in whole or in part and to make gentle comments on it: Ineke Eisberg, Ernst Beker, Wely Mazamisa, Bert Schuurman and Henk Witvliet, Sr. I am also deeply grateful to Ingrid van Geest, who has shown angelic patience in her typing. The book is dedicated to Maxim and Victor, who in the past months have too often found their father at his typewriter.

1

The Historical Context

The term 'Third World' is relatively recent; it is a generalized designation applied to all the countries on the periphery of the industrial and capitalist system of the 'First World' (the US, Western Europe, Japan, Australia and New Zealand) and the Eastern European socialism of the 'Second World'. The term suggests a unity which has never existed and does not exist even now: it denotes both the former colonial countries and even a country like China which to a large extent has been able to escape the Western sphere of influence; it embraces both the OPEC countries and the poorest countries of all; it embraces both countries with a 'free-market' economy (Brazil, Kenya, Indonesia) and socialist countries (Cuba, Mozambique, Vietnam).

However, a term like 'Third World', with the inevitable connotation of 'third-class world', did not come into currency quite by chance. It has joined terms like 'developing countries', 'poor countries', as a staple ingredient of the *(hi)story* which we tell one another about how things are out there, a long way away from us. This story, handed on by school, family, churches and media, is an ideological expression of what we imagine to be our relationship with what goes on out there. This image (ideology, cf. the Greek *eidos* = image) is not just an illusion, but at the same time it is far from giving an adequate picture of the reality to which it relates. Like all ideological elements, as the French Marxist philosopher Louis Althusser puts it, it displays a structure of understanding/misunderstanding (reconnaissance/ méconnaissance).

That means that we must remember that the story about the 'Third World' does not give us any *direct* access to its reality or to our relationship with it. Certainly it makes this reality quite recognizable, but at the same time it misunderstands and conceals the real relationship between the 'Third World' and our world.

In other words, the unthinking use of terms like 'Third World', 'developing countries' and 'poor countries' in the first place tells us something about the way in which we imagine and depict our relationship to reality there: only in the second instance does the use of these terms tell us anything about the real circumstances which underlie them, in a concealed form which calls for a critical analysis of them (and of the ideology which goes with them).

It might be asked whether a modern medium like television is not ideally capable of breaking through this disguise. At any rate, does not this medium make it possible for us to see realities in the 'Third World' with our own eyes?

Alas, precisely as a result of the sophisticated way in which television creates the illusion that the viewer really is seeing what is happening in distant countries, this medium largely contributes towards confirming existing conceptions. At any rate, in the first place the viewer does not see 'reality' there, but only what the programme makers have been willing or able to show. In the second place, the viewer's own perception is itself selective: as a rule only what can be fitted into his or her already existing world of experience will actually get through; any programme-maker who wants to show something of the other-ness of reality in countries like El Salvador or Guatemala is confronted with the almost impossible task of breaking open this already existing world of experience. A further compli-cating factor is the inevitable growth of familiarity; the 'Third World' has found its way into our homes and bedrooms and has become part of our daily reality – with all the feelings of guilt and impotence which it constantly provokes. Finally, it has to be said that while television and video can transmit pictures, they cannot transmit smell and stench; and in our experience the stench of sickness, ordure and decay is the most appalling aspect of the situation in which millions of people have to live in the shanty towns of Bombay or Calcutta. Television pictures, however horrible, give only an innocent and therefore misleading reflection of this reality.

(a) The story of poor countries

The historian J.Huizinga begins his book *The Waning of the Middle Ages* quite brilliantly, like this:

> To the world when it was half a thousand years younger, the outlines of all things seemed more clearly marked than to us. The contrast between suffering and joy, between adversity and happiness, appeared more striking. All experiences had yet to the minds of men the directness and absoluteness of the pleasure and pain of child-life. Every event, every action was still embodied in expressive and solemn forms, which raised them to the dignity of a ritual. For it was not merely the great facts of birth, marriage and death which by the sacredness of the sacrament were raised to the rank of mysteries; incidents of less importance, like a journey, a task, a visit, were equally attended by a thousand formalities: benedictions, ceremonies, formulas.
>
> Calamities and indigence were more afflicting than at present; it was more difficult to guard against them, to find solace. Illness and health presented a more striking contrast; the cold and darkness of winter were real evils. Honours and riches were relished with greater avidity and contrasted more vividly with the surrounding misery...

Huizinga is writing here about the Middle Ages, but his description of life five centuries ago can largely be applied to the picture that we have of life in the Third World now. Indeed life there is just as fierce, colourful and full of contrasts. There, in Chile and Argentina, class struggle really is the term for what is going on; here, however, we do things in a much more sophisticated way! The analogy between the picture that we have of the Middle Ages and our conception of the 'Third World' perhaps explains why people usually think that Third-World countries are backward, still undergoing a development that in the meantime we have left behind. Third-World countries are the Middle Ages of our time. They are 'developing countries', and consciously or not, the state of their development is measured by what we regard as the characteristics of modernity: progress, industrial and technological development, individual freedom, parliamentary democracy, secularization.

The analogy given above corresponds with the deeply-rooted

conception that the history of the Third-World countries is still new compared with that of Europe, the cradle of modern civilization. In most history books the continents Asia, Africa and America appear from the moment when they are 'discovered'. Their history only really begins from the time when they are integrated into the history of Western expansion and progress.

'Columbus discovered America.' This familiar sentence from school textbooks is a classic example of an ideological conception with a structure of understanding/misunderstanding. On the one hand it expresses adequately the courage, the curiosity and the sense of freedom as a result of which the 'old world', Europe, put the 'new world' on the map in the second half of the fifteenth and in the sixteenth century: it denotes the development of awareness among the middle classes, who now no longer saw the world as a closed universe but as a sphere to explore and exploit. On the other hand the statement fails to note the fact that Columbus did not discover an unknown land but land which long before had been 'discovered' by the Indians. It conceals the fact that these original inhabitants could look back on a long history of impressive achievements: at the time when the *conquistadores* came ashore, Central and Latin America had the powerful kingdoms of the Mayas, the Aztecs and the Incas, together comprising between seventy and ninety million inhabitants; one hundred and fifty years later, this number had been drastically reduced to three and a half million. 'These societies have left behind countless testimonies to their greatness despite this long period of devastation: religious monuments which were built more skilfully than the pyramids of Egypt; useful technical inventions for the struggle against nature; works of art of incomparable talent. In the museum of Lima one can see hundreds of skulls on which trepanning has been practised or to which gold and silver plates have been attached by Inca surgeons. The Mayas were great astronomers; they discovered the value of the figure zero (earlier than any other people in history). The irrigation canals and the artificial islands which the Aztecs had made left Hernando Cortes dumbfounded, even though they were not made of gold' (Eduardo Galeano).

In the period of capitalist mercantile exploitation, genocide was practised on a scale without parallel in history. Let us take

Jamaica as an example. When Columbus 'discovered' this island in 1494, he found the Arawak Indians there: their number is estimated at 60,000. By the time that the English captured Jamaica from the Spaniards in 1655, the Arawaks had been completely exterminated.

Nor should we suppose that the genocide of Indians which began then is now a thing of the past. In the Amazon territory of Brazil, Indian peoples are robbed of their land and exterminated when the interests of local and multi-national commerce (uranium!) make that necessary. In December 1976 the Brazilian Minister for Internal Affairs made the following statement: 'Within ten years we plan to reduce the total number of Indians in Brazil from 200,000 to 20,000; and within thirty years we want them all to be integrated into our national society.' While the situation in Brazil is particularly alarming, elsewhere, too, native peoples are driven from their land and forced to move to barren areas which are not conducive to their survival (South Africa, Australia, Panama, New Zealand, Canada and the Philippines).

All our lives we have been familiarized with the contrast between rich countries and poor countries. The Western countries are 'rich' and the Third-World countries are 'poor', and depend on our help. This conception, too, has the typical structure of understanding/misunderstanding. The economic standard of life is certainly low in many Third-World countries (but not all); national debts are high and the basic population of these countries is made up of farm-workers with little or no land who either try to maintain their often wretched position in the country or escape to the shanty towns of the great cities where things are often even worse. However, the contrast between rich and poor countries is not a natural contrast: the 'poor countries' are not naturally poor and the 'rich countries' are not naturally rich. The contrast has come about historically, and that is consciously or unconsciously forgotten.

The poor countries were *made* poor, and often their original riches are the cause of their present poverty. A telling example of this is Bolivia, now one of the poorest countries in the world. In 1545 silver mines were discovered in the city of Potosi which represented fabulous riches: this discovery was the beginning of enormous exports of silver from Spanish America to Europe. It is calculated that the quantity of silver which was brought to Spanish ports in something more than one hundred and fifty years was three times as great as the whole of the European reserves. Moreover, Spain itself was far from being the chief country to profit from this plundering. 'In Europe there was fierce competition to capture the Spanish market, which included the South American market and South American silver. Thanks to a French memorandum from the end of the seventeenth century we know that at this time Spain controlled only five per cent of trade with "her" colonial possessions on the other side of the ocean, despite the legalistic illusion of her monopoly: about a third of the total trade was in the hands of the Dutch and Flemish; a quarter belonged to the French; the Genoese controlled more than twenty per cent, the English ten per cent and the Germans rather less. South America was a European concern' (Eduardo Galeano).

The industrial and capitalist system which brought the West unprecedented material prosperity could come about thanks to unjust trading with and plundering of colonial territories, genocide and – it should not be forgotten – slave-trading and slavery. In 1847 Karl Marx wrote:

> Direct slavery is the lynch-pin of bourgeois industry, just like machines, etc. Without slavery there is no cotton; without cotton there is no modern industry. Only slavery has given the colonies their value; the colonies created world trade, and world trade is the prerequisite of large-scale industry. Thus slavery is an economic category of supreme importance.

Later, in the well-known twenty-fourth chapter of *Das Kapital*, Marx showed not only that the discovery of the gold and silver mines in America, the plundering of the East Indies and the slave trade are the main features in the 'so-called original accumulation' (i.e. the accumulation of capital needed to bring about the industrial and capitalist revolution) but also that the strong growth of industrialization came about at the expense of the working class in Western countries then selves. In this connection Marx says of Holland:

> Holland, which first developed the colonial system fully, had already reached its zenith as a trading nation by 1648. Holland

was 'in almost exclusive possession of trade in the East Indies and of traffic between the south-west and north-east of Europe. Its fisheries, shipping and manufacturing exceeded those of any other country. The capital resources of the republic were perhaps more extensive than those of the rest of Europe put together.'

Gülich [whom Marx is quoting here, TW] forgets to add that by 1648 the mass of Dutch people was more overworked, impoverished and brutally suppressed than that of the rest of Europe put together.

One thing is certain: there is a close historical link between the development of the West and the underdevelopment of countries in Asia, Africa, Latin-America and the Caribbean. Similarly, it is certain that the historical process which led to the contrast between 'developed' and 'underdeveloped' countries is unique and cannot be repeated. However, in the developing countries which came into being after the Second World War there was little sense of this historical process and its unique character. The tacit assumption was that the countries of the 'Third World' would have to undergo a more or less identical process of development to that on which the rich countries could look back. All that was necessary was to create the economic and social conditions for the developing countries to 'take off', the starting point for unstoppable economic growth (for more detail see chapter 6 (a) below). However, in the course of the 1950s and 1960s it became painfully evident that this form of 'development help' only led to an increase in the gulf between rich and poor countries.

In the second half of the 1960s people became aware that Western economic, political and cultural achievements should no longer be taken as a norm and criterion for developments in the 'Third World'. Terms like 'self-reliance' and 'intermediate technology' came into fashion. This process of growing awareness certainly bore fruit, and the results are expressed above all in the international discussion surrounding the Sixth (1974) and Seventh (1975) Special Sessions of the United Nations on the need for a new international economic order. However, we should not forget that in the 1980s this discussion has already become a non-issue, not least because the logic of multi-national capital constantly

seems to dictate a quite specific international economic order of
its own.

(b) The story of world mission

What part did mission play in the process of the exploration and
exploitation of the 'Third World'? The story of the advance and
triumphant progress of the gospel in the pagan world, so often
told with excitement in missionary tracts and pamphlets, has
certainly not been silenced, but it has become increasingly incredible. The success story of the 'fields white to harvest' has been
displaced by the sorry story of guilt and complicity in the extermination and exploitation of foreign peoples and cultures. However,
this latest account of mission, as a fifth column of Western
colonialism, is itself an inadequate expression of a historical
reality which is much too complex to be described in simple
generalizations.

There is much to be said for making the modern history of
mission begin at the decisive moment of the great discoveries of
America and India by the Spaniards and Portuguese in 1492-97.
Hardly a year had elapsed after Columbus set foot in America for
the first time than Pope Alexander VI, in his bull *Inter caetera
divinae* of 1493, divided the New World up between Spain and
Portugal; and he did not hesitate to describe the adventurous and
profitable enterprise in terms of the dissemination of Catholic
faith and the Christian religion. The conquest of foreign territories
had a sacred character; its aim was no less than the extension of
God's kingdom on earth.

Here we must remember that our familiar modern distinction
(even division) between the gospel itself and the way in which
Christianity has given that gospel form over the centuries (which
Protestants find easier than Catholic and Eastern Orthodox
believers) did not exist for Columbus and his contemporaries. For
them the gospel as it were coincided with the way in which it was
practised; in other words it coincided with the administration of
the sacraments, the hierarchical structures of the church and the
crusade against Islam.

The year 1492 was the year not only of the discovery of America
but also of the definitive reconquest of Spain from the Moors (and
at the same time of the expulsion of 150,000 Jews from that

country). The annexation of a new territory for the Spanish crown was seen as the fulfilment of the old Christian dream that God's salvation would extend to the ends of the earth – and this identification was expressed in the right secured by the king of Spain to nominate bishops in America.

From the beginning, the history of mission has been entangled with the history of European expansion; conversely, from the beginning the conquest of distant lands has been associated with a strongly developed sense of Christian mission.

This fact alone was to have consequences for the way in which missionary history was written. It was to make it *a priori* impossible to understand the history of mission as a special history separate from secular realities. The question of the historical and theological significance of missionary practices and ideas cannot be answered apart from a comprehensive analysis of the specific constellation of the historical circumstances in which they came about; that means that in terms of method we must understand the history of mission critically as part of history in general. However, if we look at existing missionary literature, we can see that here, much ground still needs to be broken: all we have are some first beginnings and a number of detailed studies.

Present-day missiology is intensively preoccupied with the normative question of the missionary task of the Christian community, and in answering this question it works with concepts like 'holistic approach' and 'contextualization'; however, valuable though such concepts may be in themselves, they remain in a vacuum unless they are systematically applied to the historical question of the significance and function of mission in past centuries.

The entanglement of the history of mission with colonial history poses two basic questions.

1. How far have missionary practices and ideas formed an integral part of the process of the extension of colonial and imperialist power?

2. How far has missionary activity achieved the liberation of men and women from structures of domination and dependence, in obedience to the gospel as a story of liberation from slavery?

As to the first point, the complex and often tense relationship between colonial authorities and missionaries cannot be described in a few pages. However, for our purposes it is important to establish that this very complexity also results from the fact that both parties have usually worked in more or less overlapping areas. Both were conscious of representing and disseminating Christian culture: mission and civilization went hand in hand.

The interests of church and state were tightly interwoven in the period of Iberian colonization: both were concerned to transplant the hierarchical and feudal structures of church and society to American soil as faithfully as possible (we need not concern ourselves further here with the fact that the maintenance of the feudal structure of society ultimately proved a disaster for Spain and Portugal). The papal bull of 1493 not only authorized mission by the sword, but at the same time made it virtually impossible to criticize in principle the robbery and exploitation practised by the *conquistadores*. As a result, not only the colonists, but also the missionaries, found it difficult to regard the Indians as human beings, let alone as human beings with equal rights. Granted, in his bull *Sublimis Deus* of 1536, Paul III proclaimed that Indians were 'true human beings', in a state to receive the Catholic faith and sacraments, but the very fact that such a statement was necessary proves that many people had doubts about *veri homines*.

It is difficult to find an adequate explanation of the origin of this ethnocentrism. Did not Christian faith teach that all peoples were descended from one common father, Adam, and did it not in this way acknowledge the unity of the human race? Certainly, but that is not the whole story: in the Conquistadores proclamation of 1513, made by the crown lawyer Palacios Rubios and approved by the Council for India, it was asserted that while all peoples indeed descend from Adam and Eve, God put the rule over all peoples in the hands of one man, the Pope of Rome, who in turn had given the newly discovered worlds to the Spanish crown; the Indians had to accept the rule of the Spanish king and be converted to the true religion, on pain of subjugation by force and slavery. Furthermore, while the books of the Bible and the church fathers offered material from which to argue in theory that the Indians were inferior, here the Greek philosopher Aristotle offered a way out: his theory of human hierarchy served as a basis for the argument in which the humanist Juan Ginés de Sepúlveda stressed that the Indian is by nature a slave, inferior to the European, who is by nature his master.

De Sepúlveda's theory is no more than a rational justification of the already existing European sense of superiority. It does not explain its origin. In all probability at least three factors contributed to the development of European ethnocentrism. First of all, dawning awareness at the Renaissance, through scientific discoveries and the great voyages of exploration, which among other things uncovered dazzling mineral wealth, had an overwhelming effect. Secondly, their sense of superiority meant that the Europeans came to the new world as defenders of true religion, called by God to Christianize the heathen. Finally, the Europeans came as conquerors, thanks to their superior technology (gunpowder, iron, etc.) which made it possible for them to defeat great armies of Indians with a small number of men.

However, in the period of Iberian colonialism the church also had another face. In the sixteenth and seventeenth centuries there was a constant undercurrent of missionary opposition to the exploitation and murder of Indians. Here mention must be made of Dominicans like Antonio de Montesinos, Pedro de Córdoba and Bartolomé de Las Casas, and also the Jesuit villages or 'reducciones', as they are called (protected Indian settlements governed by missionaries), in seventeenth-century Paraguay (which was not entirely contiguous with the present-day state of that name).

For present-day Latin-American theologians, Bartolomé de Las Casas above all is a prophet of liberation. He came to the New World in 1502, and his discontent over the treatment of the Indians grew to such an extent that in 1514 he abandoned his *encomedienda* (the estate, with the Indians resident on it, which was assigned to conquerors) and from then on devoted himself wholly to the defence of the native population. In the dispute with J.G. de Sepúlveda he maintained that the Indians were not only Adam's descendants but also had the right to be treated as free men and women. For de Las Casas, salvation was indissolubly bound up with social justice, so he believed that not only the salvation of the 'unbelievers', the Indians, was in danger, but that of the 'believers', the Spaniards, who practised robbery, murder and plunder! In 1542 de Las Casas succeeded in having the 'New Laws' for the protection of the Indian population accepted, but the repeal of them in 1545 by Charles V represented final failure for his work. Looking back on it, he could say: 'I left behind me in the Indies Jesus Christ our God, scourged, tortured, crucified, not once but a million times.'

Still, even de Las Casas was not without his weaknesses: in 1516 he proposed the introduction of black slaves in order to spare the Indians; he was later to regret this proposal deeply. Nevertheless he remains an exceptional figure for his time, because he appreciated the distinctive characteristics of the Indians as having value in their own right (thus Enrique Dussel). At the beginning of the period of European expansion he contrasted the God of conquerors and oppressors with the God of the Bible, the God who takes the side of the humiliated and the oppressed.

As to the close connection between Christianity and Western culture, the spread of the Catholic faith remained remarkably consistent in character over the course of time. Even in the eighteenth century, when the French missionaries were predominant, mission continued to serve to transplant hierarchical church structures to foreign soil.

A breakthrough in the view that the aim of mission was to extend the church as a hierarchical institution in fact only became possible when Vatican II relativized the institutional approach in favour of the dynamic conception of the 'people of God', thus stressing the participation and responsibility of all Christians in the *missio Dei* (God's mission).

However, the presence of tensions and conflicts is evident from the emergence of a number of Jesuit missionaries who sought to adopt the native culture and were the first to form theories of comparative religion. The best known among them is Matteo Ricci (1552-1610), a famous astronomer and geographer, who mastered the Chinese language, philosophy and culture before looking for converts. His accommodation to Confucian conceptions and rites was the occasion for the well-known 'rites dispute', which only ended in 1742 with a definitive prohibition of accommodation by Pope Benedict XIV.

One might expect that the Protestant mission, which in fact

only really got going in the eighteenth century, would have had less difficulty in distinguishing between Christian belief and European culture and civilization. Was not the Protestant mission in the seventeenth and eighteenth centuries primarily supported by Puritanism and pietistic communities, who were keenly aware of the discontinuity between God's Word and the externals of church authority and tradition? Had not the Puritan emigrants broken with the past, and were they not pilgrims on the way to the promised land of Canaan that God was to show them, in order to build a new society there in accordance with his Word?

In practice, though, these elect did not behave very differently towards the Indians from the Catholic missionaries before them. Here the Calvinist doctrine of election was of decisive significance. When the Pilgrim Fathers began a new life in Massachusetts in 1620, to begin with they went out to meet the native population quite openly. Whereas the Spaniards simply took land from the Indians, the Puritans tried to make contracts of purchase with them in a democratic way. However, it soon transpired that the Indians did not understand democracy and did not keep to agreements freely made (they continued to regard the land as their own property); moreover, it emerged that they did not farm their land like good tenants and made little progress along the road of Christian salvation. So the elect could only draw the conclusion that they were confronted with a rejected people who were an example of the negative aspect of divine predestination: the extermination of this people was in accord with God's unfathomable counsel.

If the Reformation represents the discovery (or rediscovery) of Christian freedom, among the emigrants driven from their homeland this freedom was primarily focussed on Christian faith as a faith of free people; however, it did not lead to the discovery of the freedom of others and their right to be valued in their distinctive otherness.

As in Latin America, so too in New England there was deep concern about the lot of the Indian. John Eliot must be mentioned here, among others. He began his mission among the Indians in 1646. In it, baptism was not the first but the last phase of the process of conversion: his work aimed at the establishment of Indian colonies, and he received support from

England from the first Protestant missionary society to be founded, in 1649, i.e. The Society for the Propagation of the Gospel in New England.

If the Catholic mission in the period of Iberian colonialism is set against the background of a feudal society of an agrarian kind, the background to missionary activities from Protestant countries was the rise of bourgeois capitalist society. The significance of Puritanism in the rise of the industrial revolution is known well enough. In this Calvinistic variant of Protestantism, freedom is the freedom of those who are capable of earning interest on their talents and whose social success is a sign of God's gracious guidance in their lives, since God helps ordinary, independent people who are able to help themselves. Already among Puritan leaders like Cromwell and John Milton we see that the idea of election becomes a national concern: Cromwell quoted to Parliament Isaiah's prophecy, 'The people I have formed for myself shall proclaim my praise' (43.21), substituting England for ancient Israel: the English people is the elect people with a special mission in world history. In this way the seventeenth-century Puritans contributed to the development of a national consciousness of mission, which not only legitimated but also stimulated a colonialist and imperialist extension of power. Of course England was not alone in this development. In other European countries, too, the growth of an industrial capitalistic society went hand in hand with the rise of an aggressively nationalistic sense of mission: it is only a step from 'Rule, Britannia, Britannia rule the waves, Britons never shall be slaves', composed in 1740, to E.Geibel's line, 'Und es soll am deutschen Wesen einmal die Welt gewesen' (One day the whole world will be German). When the period of imperialism began, round about 1870, both the expansion of the world market through colonial wars and increasing conflicts between nations were bolstered by a nationalistic sense of mission, which we can confidently call cultural messianism.

Mission could not avoid the vortex of this messianism. The missionary charge in Matt.28.19 was at the same time a command to bring the colonized peoples into contact with the achievements of European culture. However, that does not mean that the missionaries were tied to the leading strings of the colonial powers.

On the contrary, many of them were aware of the devastating effect of economic and political self-interest on the fortunes of colonized peoples and cultures. Still, this made the task of civilizing these peoples all the more urgent; only in this way could the damage of the white lust for power and desire for gain be limited. We must read against this background the following sentences written in 1879 by the German pioneer in missiology, Gustav Warneck: 'In making the pagans Christians, mission also makes them real human beings, and in implanting the kingdom of God among them it also implants true culture. Culture is not the main aim of mission, but its necessary consequence, a free gift, a by-product, a blessing which falls to the earth from the rich table of the gospel.'

For Warneck, cultural work may not be the main aim of the Christian mission but a necessary consequence, but things change when in nineteenth-century German liberal theology the absoluteness of Christianity becomes problematical. In that case the cultural task becomes the chief aim. The liberal theologian, philosopher and sociologist of religion Ernst Troeltsch would have nothing to do with mass conversions or pietistic missions concerned to save souls. But in an article, 'Mission in the Modern World', written in 1906, he regards mission as a duty for Christian peoples; it is of universal importance to European and American culture, for no more and no less is at stake than the idea of *Kulturmenschheit*. Troeltsch ends his article like this:

Neither fanaticism nor compassion should lead us to think that we must force our religion on all peoples. But we remain certain that in conjunction with the ancient civilization of Europe, the Christian religion is the supreme form and power of spiritual life, despite all the faults, conflicts and impurities in our civilization.

Therefore we feel ourselves obliged and justified in intervening with our higher possession wherever higher and better things seek to be formed or must be formed... So mission, too, continues to be a matter of public concern, no matter what criticisms people may have of it. It is a matter of course for the British. It is to be hoped that we Germans too, who are only slowly becoming aware of world horizons, will understand that mission is not just something for enthusiasts and the strict church groups, but is a matter of public concern for our people.

What Troeltsch is expressing here on the eve of the First World War is far more than a personal vision. There may perhaps have been differences of opinion over the utility of mission, but there was considerable unanimity over the conception of a world culture along the lines of Western social structures, even among those who would have nothing to do with the popular social Darwinist theories of race which were so popular at this time. Development and progress were thought to be products of European culture and history, and only those people had a real history who played a part in *this* history, which was history *par excellence* (in fact there was no other). Only the catastrophe of two world wars on the one hand and confrontation with the process of the emancipation of the 'Third-World' countries succeeded in shaking this deep-rooted cultural messianism.

The theory and practice of mission experienced the far-reaching consequences of this last development. In order to remedy the fragmentation and lack of coordination in Protestant mission, a series of World Mission Conferences have been held during the course of the twentieth century (Edinburgh 1910, Jerusalem 1928, Tambaram 1938, Whitby 1947, Willingen 1953, Achimota 1957, Mexico City 1963, Bangkok 1972/73 and Melbourne 1980). They are a good indication of the changes which have taken place. Whereas the 1910 Edinburgh Conference with its slogan 'The evangelization of the world in this generation' took for granted as its starting-point the coincidence of mission and civilization, in Jerusalem 1928 the relationship of Christianity to other religions became an explicit topic of discussion. Gradually people became open to a concept of mission in which mission was not seen exclusively as geographically determined one-way traffic from the West to other parts of the world. In Mexico City 1963 it was affirmed that all six continents are in principle mission fields; the churches throughout the world are in a missionary situation and need to provide mutual support for one another to fulfil the one missionary task. Mission is no longer an activity which the churches carry on elsewhere, but a key concept which relates to the presence of the church in the world (the fact that it is sent); instead of being a quantitative concept, in which the main concern is the number of people who are reached by the message of the gospel, mission becomes a qualitative concept relating to the way in which the church is present and takes sides in specific social conditions. In Bangkok 1972/73, where representatives of the 'young churches' were in the majority for the first time, there was sharp criticism of the one-sided way in which the term 'salvation' was understood by the Western churches. There was a plea for a comprehensive approach, capable of breaking through the Western dualism of body and spirit, thought and action, theory and practice. Finally, the 1980 Melbourne conference developed this vision of a 'holistic mission' in the direction of a 'church of the poor'.

As to the second point mentioned above, anyone who notes the way in which mission is entangled with forms of colonial and imperialist rule will in the first instance be inclined to conclude that in the traditional mission field the original story of the liberation brought by Jesus the Messiah has become a story of oppression and alienation. However, in fact things are considerably more complicated. In this connection it is worth listening to M.M.Thomas, the former Chairman of the Central Committee of the World Council of Churches. At the World Missionary Conference in Bangkok in 1972/73 he gave a speech in which he expressly called attention to the liberating aspects of mission in his own country, India.

Christian missions have preached to the tribals and villagers the deliverance of the human spirit from the domination of the 'elemental spirits of the universe' peopling the sun, moon and stars, mountains, trees and rocks, and from the fatalism of poverty; it has sought to shift sacredness from the cow and other animals to the human person; it has grappled with the spiritual demon behind the caste-system and challenged communities with the reality of the eucharistic fellowship, transcending caste; it has broken the spiritual halo around the species of idolatrous asceticism which tended to consider abstinence in matters of food and sex as an instrument of salvation. The prophetic tradition helped the shift from ceremonial purity to righteousness in historical existence.

Of course M.M.Thomas is very well aware of the other side of the coin. The Western idols have often drowned out the voice of the biblical prophets. Nevertheless, mission has had the effect of demythologizing, making possible a development towards a more humane and just society.

In the ferment of the Asian revolution which is still in progress, M.M.Thomas, following Gandhi, looks for a connection between elements which have come from the West to India (equality, individual freedom, democracy) and elements from original Indian culture and tradition.

What applies to India need not necessarily apply to other countries in Asia, Africa or Latin America. The process of political, economic, religious and cultural domination has taken very different courses in each of these countries. Only a contextual analysis can give a reply to the question what mission means and can still mean for a specific country or territory.

(c) The other story

This section could also have had the title 'I spy with my little eye...', but the seeing involved here has none of the innocence of the familiar game; on the contrary, it implies the end of innocence, that pseudo-innocence where the dominant ideology, the ideology of those in a position of domination, constantly seems to overlook the terrors and the injustices the guilt for which it shares.

We return once again to the dispute between Bartolomé de Las Casas and Juan Ginés de Sepúlveda. The latter supported his dogmatic argument with a mass of quotations and clothed it with the authority of tradition. The refutation by de Las Casas is characterized by equally subtle distinctions and a wealth of quotations, but he begins his argument with a sentence which in fact breaks through the academic, learned character of the discussion and rules the position of his opponent out of court on the basis of what is actually happening. According to de Las Casas, the consequence of his opponent's position is 'the loss of countless human lives and the depopulation of more than two thousand miles of land'. The Peruvian theologian Gustavo Gutiérrez has rightly indicated the methodological significance of this statement: for de Las Casas, the criterion of truth in theological argument does not lie in the theoretical argumentation but in its practical effect and consequences. De Sepúlveda and others take no account of these consequences, for their intellectualism obscures their view of reality: they do not *see* the Indian.

By contrast Bartolomé de Las Casas certainly saw the suffering of the Indian, and in the light of the evidence of this blatant injustice he could no longer talk in abstractions. He could no longer think it away. Thought cannot go behind this evidence, pigeon-holing it and thus making it harmless and innocent. Starting from the evident reality of suffering and injustice, thought can only analyse and investigate how it can happen. For de Las Casas, however, this intellectual work is not a separate activity, but a necessary part of his praxis, his commitment.

What moved Bartolomé de Las Casas to this commitment? What moved him to take sides with a despised human race and to make the protection of this slave people his life's work? Seeing the Indian meant far more to brother Bartolomé than the empirical perception of suffering, pain and injustice. Behind the evidence of the slavery and exploitation of the people he saw more deep-seated evidence: the manifestation of the God of the poor, the revelation of the crucified Christ. He saw in the Indian the presence of the other (indeed the Other), and this presence drove him to his commitment. This more deep-seated evidence cannot be verified empirically; on the contrary, it is diametrically opposed to what 'people' think to be natural and take for granted, namely that since he is the almighty, 'God' identifies himself with the powerful. Far less is this evidence the result of an autonomous process of thought; on the contrary, it goes against all logic which extrapolates from what exists (and how can logic be constructed except from what is?). The evidence in question here is evidence given in faith, 'the certainty that one hopes for and the proof of things unseen' (Heb.11.1); in dogmatic terms, like the praxis which sets it in motion and keeps it alive, it is an aspect of the doctrine of the Holy Spirit.

That Bartolomé de Las Casas sees the Indian as the poor in terms of the gospel makes him a model for present-day liberation theologians. De Sepúlveda missed this insight because his theorizing as a theologian was not embedded in a praxis of discipleship. For de Las Casas, by contrast, praxis was part of the way in which he acquired theological knowledge, and this methodological intuition makes him so important for theologians like Gutiérrez and Dussel, for whom the 'non-persons' (people who are thought to have no culture and no history) are the focus of theological concern in the present-day situation of Latin America – as they were for de Las Casas in the sixteenth century. For De Sepúlveda, the God of the Christians had his place in the story of spectacular conquests and successes; the Indians were simply unbelieving pagans who had to be converted. By contrast, Bartolomé de Las Casas knew another story: for him a living pagan Christian was better than a dead Christian Indian, for his God was the crucified Christ who identifies himself with the poor. For him, the dividing line did not run between Christians and pagans, believers and unbelievers, but between oppressed and oppressors, between life and death.

This seeing of the other (Other) is equally central in a long pastoral letter which was published on 6 May 1973. It was written by six bishops from Central-West Brazil about the situation of the farm-workers in the diocese of Goiás. The document is impressive simply by virtue of the great simplicity and clarity with which it is written. Its description of the circumstances of the people whose lives the bishops share bears witness to great care and attention to detail; nothing is exaggerated, everything is quantified: instruction, feeding, hygiene, health care, income, opportunities for work (or rather unemployment), social security (or rather total insecurity). The conclusion is unambiguous: 'So this is the situation of the people in the country, as black as the night outside, but at the same time it is a situation in which human values shine out all the brighter; none of these difficulties prevents people from struggling and persevering in a task which, far from freeing workers from their poverty, serves to make the rich even richer.'

The bishops compare this life with a fruit tree. When a tree bears bad fruit, it is necessary to discover why, to investigate the state of the roots and the ground. Once the cause is found, an attempt is made to treat it. But what if the tree does not get better despite all these attempts? What if the tree seems thoroughly rotten? In that case it has to be uprooted and another tree has to be planted which does bear good fruit.

The bishops' metaphor is clear. In their diocese the tree is fatally diseased. But what are the causes? To find that out it is necessary to look at the roots of the tree, i.e. the organization of the structures of production in the countryside. The bishops come to the conclusion that these too seem to be seriously affected by the disease. Ownership of land is divided very unequally: most peasants are seasonal workers and have no land; they are dependent on individual estate owners who own so much land that they often no longer know precisely how much they do have (moreover, they live a long way away, in the great cities). Nor is this situation characteristic only of the diocese of Goiás; it is characteristic of the whole Brazil countryside. This discovery leads the bishops to pursue their investigation further and to look at the ground in which the tree is planted: the social and economic situation of Brazil. They give an accurate survey of both the government's agricultural policy and the way in which Brazilian capitalism functions. The conclusion is inevitable: 'The history of our people, our history, is the history of the marginalization of human beings. What does that mean? It means that the great majority of people have never had the possibility of sharing in decision making: not in any decisions at all, in politics, in the economy, or even in the church. They have always been forced to listen, to carry out the decisions of others (some others)... We speak of marginalization, not just of marginalized people. To return once again to the story of the tree with which we began: the marginalized are the fruits; marginalization is what makes the tree produce bad fruits. In the present situation the tree is none other than our society, our economy, our church, which has functioned in such a way that it has forced countless people to the margin of existence, has excluded them, has marginalized them.'

The bishops have not come to this conclusion by way of academic analysis. Of course in their investigation they have made use of the means that modern science puts at their disposal. But their point of reference lies elsewhere. It lies in what they see and hear, every day, of the people with whom they are in touch. Their pastoral responsibility has gradually taught them to see the world through the eyes of the marginalized about whom we see them speaking in their letter. They do not go back on this experience. Their analysis begins from evidence, which certainly calls for, indeed cries out for, further clarification and analysis (precisely because it is so unbelievable!) but which need not itself be subjected to further discussion or justification. For however unwelcome this evidence may be to those in power, it is visible to those who have eyes to see and can be quantified by anyone who takes the trouble to do so.

Whereas for the most part the letter consists of description and analysis of a situation of social injustice which has become evident to the bishops, at the end we suddenly find another sort of evidence, the evidence of an experience of faith which forms the source of inspiration for their thought and action. Just as Bartolomé de Las Casas recognized the crucified Christ in the face of the Indians, so the bishops recognize the people of God in the marginalized people of their diocese. 'With our eyes and with our ears we see and hear people day after day. And as we go about our life we are busy trying to understand that this people is the Good News of Christ for the world, for Brazil. The people does not regard this world as its "abiding dwelling place" (St Paul). This is not a settled people. It does not lose courage. It believes. It hopes. No single social category and no single social class has so great a thirst for justice and so great a longing for liberation.'

Anyone who ignores this experience of faith ignores the essence of liberation theology. As theoretical reflection, liberation theology is critical thinking against the background of a praxis nurtured by this experience of faith. This experience – far removed from the individualized and privatized petty-bourgeois experience against which Karl Barth spoke out so fiercely – is the primary element, though there are others. That is what liberation theologians mean when they talk about theology as 'the second step', 'the second element'. Critical reflection, conceptual thought, is not the starting point. Liberation theology does not derive its originality from its methodological contribution to the relationship between theory and praxis, contextuality, or theology as a criticism of ideology. However important these considerations may be in themselves, they are secondary to another element, the evidence of marginalized people, of their struggle for the most basic human rights, and the presence of the crucified and risen Messiah in their midst. Hugo Assmann expresses this in his own way when he says:

The starting point of liberation theology is that the painful experience of the fact that basic needs remain unfulfilled is the most important thing. Of course that also includes the need to fight for these needs to be properly supplied. The fight is just, real and normal and needs no further justification. Although 'theology' can be useful as a 'second act', as critical reflection on praxis in order to 'break down resistance', it is not a motivation for this fight, nor does it seek to be. On the contrary, it becomes free as theology, i.e. as the possibility of valid and relevant discussion of the 'word of life' (cf. I John 1) by consistently taking the side of the people in their struggle against anti-life.

2

The Epistemological Break

Looking back, we can see that it was no historical coincidence that round about 1970, forms of liberation theology developed independently of one another in different places in the world. The 1960s were years of economic growth, technological innovation and heightened expectation; for the first time in history a world without hunger and poverty was 'technically' conceivable and capable of being realized. In church life the dynamic élan of these years found expression in the pressure for renewal from the Second Vatican Council with its *aggiornamento* (adaptation) to modern society and in the favourable voyage of the ecumenical ship, buoyed up on the favourable tide by a 'theology of hope' (Jürgen Moltmann).

However, while there is the technical possibility of eliminating hunger and poverty, in reality the poor in the Third World are becoming steadily poorer and the rich even richer. The expansion of the world economy – of *this* world economy – led to the increasing impoverishment of people in the slums and villages of large parts of Asia, Africa and Latin America. At the same time, however, in the 1960s there was increasing 'conscientization' (Paulo Freire) of the proletariat of the Third World: farm-workers in the Philippines, colonized peoples in southern Africa, men and women in the shanty towns of Santiago and Lima became aware that poverty and misery are not an unchangeable fate allotted by nature but the result of structures of domination and dependence which have grown up through history and are therefore capable of change. There was a revolutionary development which also involved people who recognized the reality of the crucified and risen Christ in the sufferings and struggle of the oppressed.

In liberation theology it is of the utmost importance to recognize that this commitment of faith *precedes* the origin of any theological reflection which seeks to explain and legitimate this commitment by reference to scripture, tradition and the world church. The insight that theology is a 'second step' – first achieved and methodically developed by Latin American theologians and then recognized as a hermeneutical principle and taken over by theologians in other continents – is therefore not just a theoretical notion but an actual description of historical developments: just as Latin American liberation theology was preceded by the struggle of priests and 'laity' for radical change, so in the United States black theology arose in the context of the Civil Rights Movement and Black Power; and just as feminist theology has its setting in women's movements, so Minjung theology in Korea was born out of a years-long political struggle by Christian students, farm-workers, labourers, writers and theologians against a harsh dictatorial régime.

(a) A new way of doing theology

We saw that the most important impulse towards the rise of liberation theology came from 'seeing' the liberating reality of God in the struggle and suffering of the poor – against all the empirical evidence! However, that ignores the fact that progressive tendencies in European theology from the 1960s onwards were also influential. It would be foolish not to note that here. There is a clear line from the *aggiornamento* of Vatican II, through the decisive conference of bishops at Medellin (1968), to the publications of Latin-American theologians like Gutiérrez, Leonardo Boff, J.L.Segundo and others. Western preoccupation with the world come of age and Bonhoeffer's tentative hints at a non-religious interpretation of the Bible found its way to South Africa and South Korea. Barth, Tillich and Moltmann are emphatically present in James H.Cone's *Black Theology and Black Power*, while the political theology of Metz and Moltmann has been taken up by Latin-American liberation theology to such a degree that Moltmann can even ask critically what is really original and Latin American in this theology.

Yet on this point Jürgen Moltmann overlooked an essential difference. The theology on which he comments at the same time has another perspective and other terms of reference, however difficult European theologians seem to find this to recognize. Despite its social criticism of society, the basic problem with which modern Western theology deals continues to be that of *aggiornamento* to modernity, to the modern consciousness which developed out of the Enlightenment and which coincides historically with the growth of bourgeois capitalist society. Modern theology derives its modernity from the fact that it takes seriously the questions asked by man come of age about the possibility of belief, and weighs up the chances for the survival of Christian belief in a world in which the concept of God has become a superfluous working hypothesis. Its terms of reference are and remain those of modern society; and as long as it is at best sour grapes to assert that this society is post-capitalist and post-bourgeois, it will be extremely difficult to follow J.B.Metz in getting 'beyond bourgeois religion'.

However, when we are concerned with authentic liberation theology, in other words with a theology which can implement its commitment to a programme of liberation, we are moving in a different world, a world in which the questions and experiences of the poor and those without possessions have the highest priority. Gutiérrez puts the dividing line like this: 'Modern theology tries to answer the challenge of the "non-believer"; by contrast, liberation theology listens to the challenging questions of the "non-person".' The contrast outlined here goes far beyond the world of theological thought; it is rooted in the specific reality of domination and dependence, of the struggle over class, race and sex. The position adopted by liberation theologians calls for profound reflection on this difference in social context and on the methodological questions which it raises. The Chilean theologian Pablo Richard rightly told European theologians and church leaders that liberation theology does not present any new themes, but is a new way of doing theology. It is not just reflection on the *concept* of liberation; it is concerned with the way in which theology can have a liberating function, or, to put it more accurately, in which theology can function in a praxis of liberation. That is the real challenge of this theology with its methodological and hermeneutical questions and insights.

This challenge is clearly expressed in the Final Declaration of the First Assembly of EATWOT which took place in Dar-es-

Salaam, Tanzania, in 1976. Theologians from Asia, Africa and Latin America agreed on the following statement:

> The theologies from Europe and North America are dominant today in our churches and represent one form of cultural domination. They must be understood to have arisen out of situations related to those countries, and therefore must not be uncritically adopted without our raising the question of their relevance in the context of our countries. Indeed we must, in order to be faithful to the gospel and to our peoples, reflect on the realities of our own situations and interpret the Word of God in relation to those realities. We reject as irrelevant an academic type of theology that is divorced from action. We are prepared for a radical break in epistemology which makes commitment the first act of theology and engages in critical reflection on the praxis of the reality of the Third World...
>
> We call for an active commitment to the promotion of justice and the prevention of exploitation, the accumulation of wealth in the hands of a few, racism, sexism and all other forms of oppression, discrimination and dehumanization. Our conviction is that the theologian should have a fuller understanding of living in the Holy Spirit, for this also means being committed to a life-style of solidarity with the poor and the oppressed and involvement in action with them. Theology is not neutral. In a sense all theology is committed, conditioned notably by the socio-cultural context in which it is developed. The Christian theological task in our countries is to be self-critical of the theologians' conditioning by the value system of their environment. It has to be seen in relation to the need to live and work with those who cannot help themselves, and to be with them in their struggle for liberation.

In this important part of the Final Declaration three basic methodological questions are raised. Although they can be distinguished from one another, they nevertheless overlap: 1. the question of contextuality; 2. the relationship between theory and praxis; 3. the the criticism of ideology.

1. Contextuality

In the Final Declaration from Dar-es-Salaam it was asserted that the uncritical transfer of theology from Europe and North

America alienates people in the Third World from their situation, and in this way represents a form of cultural domination. The text does not investigate in detail why this is the case, but at all events it makes a connection with the academic character of this theology, in other words with the way it is rooted in an idealistic and rationalistic scientific way of thinking which gives it a supposedly universal validity. However, this universalist aura prevents it from taking up experiences of faith from outside its own context. As a result, in practice this absolutizing of a particular context comes close to marginalizing and despising the experiences of others.

The text further suggests that this supposedly universalist validity is achieved in this academic way of doing theology by putting thought and action, doctrine and life, dogmatics and ethics in two separate compartments. The idealistic character of this theology is closely connected with its dualism, which makes commitment, actual practice, a secondary matter. Contextual theology is above all a challenge to this dualism, a challenge rooted in both biblical theology and epistemology. In no way does it seek to exchange the particularism of traditional forms of theology for the particularism of indigenous forms. Contextuality is focussed on the whole: it is that form of theology which sees the otherness of the other (the Other), and in so doing at the same time recognizes its own social and cultural limitations. It represents a way of doing theology which is not afraid of the tension between particularity and universality, between history and eschatology.

An important contribution to the discussion on contextuality has been made by the Theological Education Fund (now renamed the Programme on Theological Education) of the World Council of Churches under the leadership of Shoki Coe, a theologian from Taiwan. In 1973, Shoki Coe published an important article in which he criticized the attempts at the 'indigenization' and 'Africanization' of theology and preaching the gospel which had been made in the 1960s. He argues that 'indigenization' is a static concept which is orientated on the past. This attempt, however, comes near to looking for a connection between two unchangeable entities, the gospel and indigenous culture. Shoki Coe contrasts indigenization with the concept of contextuality, which he describes as 'the critical assessment of what makes the context really significant in the light of the *Missio Dei*. It is the missiological discernment of the signs of the times, seeing where God is at work and calling on us to participate in that work.' However, this prophetic task of discerning the signs of the times is only possible through committed involvement in specific historical movements and situations. According to biblical theology, this last is implied by the specific character of God's revelation: the incarnation, the way in which the Word was made flesh, in a particular place and at a particular time, calls for specific discipleship: here 'specific' means a discipleship which reckons with the fact that God's Son did not take the form of abstract human nature but of a slave (Phil.2.7). 'That gospel which proclaimed the God who was concerned for all men and women at the same time had a cutting edge, precisely by being a gospel for the poor, the oppressed, the prisoners and the neglected.'

Contextuality goes much further than a recognition that all theological language is socially and culturally conditioned – though an awareness of the way in which it is conditioned by social relationships and interests remains a first requirement of contextual theology. Contextuality presupposes a creative interaction between the reading of scripture and the reading of present-day social reality: however, the mediating authority between these two elements is not the theologian as an autonomous thinker but the praxis of a community in which Christian faith is not a doctrine to be accepted but a way to be followed. This last observation calls for a more detailed account of the relationship between theory and praxis.

2. *Theory and praxis*

The theologians in Dar-es-Salaam who declare themselves ready for a radical epistemological break with an academic form of theology which is divorced from action are not primarily motivated by epistemological reasons; nor are they motivated by biblical theology. They speak above all on the basis of an experience which each had to undergo individually, the experience of the gulf between the insights and values they had obtained during their theological training and their experience of the people whom they met in their actual work. Actual experience of the gulf between theory and practice led these theologians to reflect on the possibility of bridging it.

However, while this bridging is something on which the theologian can and must reflect, reflection is possible only because the unity of thought and action, theory and practice, is already given in the divine Logos (word/deed) itself, which is above all an event: the word *happens*, it comes to us as an action which speaks and as a word which intervenes. The Logos with which the biblical narrative is concerned is the praxis of liberation, a praxis of liberation which is not shut up in a story two thousand years in the past, from which it must be distilled by the skills of modern intellectuals and then adapted to today's reality, but a praxis which is effective today and takes sides in what we call history. That is why Gutiérrez, Míguez Bonino and others describe theology as 'critical reflection on a praxis of liberation'; and the reality of this praxis precedes reflection on the possibility of it. The point of reference for liberation theology (call it dogmatic if you will) is the effective presentation of the messianic reality in the struggle and suffering of oppressed people. However, the primacy of praxis, of this praxis, makes reflection anything but superfluous. On the contrary, however true it may be that the truth of this praxis only demonstrates itself in specific discipleship, critical reflection is a necessary element within this praxis of discipleship. How can it be otherwise? This truth is so much the opposite of what we find natural and take for granted that it requires, indeed cries out for, closer interpretation and reflection. All that is evident in the empirical sense is the deep ambivalence of any revolutionary process – does not history demonstrate in abundance that all revolutions devour their children? Liberation theology is certainly not a theology which exchanges reflection for action. On the contrary, the evidence of faith which forces itself on the intellect produces such great tensions that only the community of believers, rather than the individual believer, can cope with it.

3. Criticism of ideology

However, is there not the danger that the primacy of praxis will dominate to such an extent that no room is left for the critical function of reflection? Is not contextual theology faced with the danger that the context will ultimately begin to predominate over the text of the Bible? There is no avoiding the fact that such a risk is always present. However, the question is whether this risk justifies our ignoring the insights which liberation theologians have developed in connection with contextuality. We must not lose sight of the fact that the 'hermeneutical suspicion' (an expression from the French philosopher Paul Ricoeur, taken over by Segundo and Míguez Bonino) which made the liberation theologians reach for the words of the 'masters of suspicion', Marx, Freud and Nietzsche, arose when they discovered that in the prevalent history of theology the context in fact did constantly dominate the text. The cause – at least one of the causes – of the domination of the context over a defenceless text is that even where the theologian did not just read the Bible but also the newspaper, he made the connection between the two 'from above', from what he thought to be an autonomous position. However, the Final Declaration of Dar-es-Salaam requires theologians in Third-World countries (and why not us, too?) to come down from their intellectual thrones and also ask themselves the ideological-critical question *cui bono?*. For whose benefit am I doing this? On whose behalf am I functioning?

Following the Italian Marxist Antonio Gramsci, liberation theology often talks of the theologian as an 'organic intellectual' in the service of despised groups, exploited classes and forgotten cultures. However, according to the Final Declaration, only those who are critical of the way in which they have been conditioned by milieu and environment, and question not only their own ways of thinking but also their own way of life, can function in this way.

(b) Break and continuity

In the meantime it may have become clear from what has already been said that the 'radical break in the theory of knowledge' has nothing to do with a cheap anti-intellectualism. In this connection the generalized condemnation of 'academic theology' or 'the Western tradition' which we often find in liberation theologians should not mislead us. As is always the case, here too communication is impossible without a degree of simplification. Liberation theologians know very well that there is no such thing as 'academic theology' or 'European theology'. They are well aware that the Christian tradition is interpreted and articulated in different ways within the walls of Western universities and colleges, and that there is a constant dispute over the right way to read the biblical narrative. Therefore liberation theologians can accept invitations to be visiting lecturers or to receive honorary doctorates, especially as such invitations offer the possibility of direct involvement in a dispute which is carried on not only outside but also within theological faculties.

Liberation theologians were not the first to criticize the connection between the dominant theological tradition and a rationalistic concept of science. In his farewell lectures in 1961/1962, the academic theologian Karl Barth repeated an insight that he had put into words many times earlier when he said: 'Ever since the fading of its illusory splendour as a leading power during the Middle Ages, theology has taken too many pains to justify its own existence. It has tried too hard, especially during the nineteenth century, to secure for itself at least a small but honourable place in the sun, basking in the rays of science, in order to justify its existence. This attempt at self-justification has been no help to it.' And when in 1975 Barth's pupil Helmut Gollwitzer in turn came to give his farewell lectures, he made a connection between the dominant scientific way of thinking to which theology has adapted itself and an age-old historical development in which the principle of sharing work both in church and society led to a division between a small, socially privileged stratum of learned people and experts on the one hand and the great ignorant, immature masses on the other. There is a growing awareness within university theology (though it is often still peripheral) that the context and identity of theological study is in tension with an ideal of knowledge which holds to the myth of the 'free-ranging intelligence' (Karl Mannheim) and a division between thought (which comes first) and action (which follows). While in Third-World countries liberation theology represents a minority position and the theological exports of Europe and North America are still dominant, in the West, both inside and outside academic institutions, there is growing discontent with a way of theologizing which separates thinking and living, reflection and involvement. If the problem of contextuality keeps being taken seriously, then there can be reciprocal recognition and involvement despite the difference in situation – at any rate, even as practised in the university, contextual theology is a theology 'from below': it is directed polemically against a timeless proclamation of the gospel which ignores specific social conflicts and in so doing plays into the hands of those in power.

It is therefore a misunderstanding to think that liberation theologians from the Third World reject academic or European theology outright. Academic theology and contextual theology, European theology and Third-World theology are not monolithic blocks, one confronting the other. However, precisely because misunderstandings arise here, it makes sense to look again more closely at the epistemology with which the theologians in Dar-es-Salaam want to make a break. In the readiness for a 'radical break in epistemology' we can distinguish three themes: one from biblical theology, one from epistemology and one from the criticism of ideology.

In terms of biblical theology there is a close connection between the knowledge of God and discipleship: it is a question of doing the truth (cf. John 3.21; I John 1.6), of walking in the truth (II John 4; III John 3). Liberation theology breaks with an epistemology in which God is objectivized in thought and becomes the object of abstract speculation. God is only known from the reality of his *debarim* (words/acts), and the history of these *debarim* is only known from the specific act of discipleship: *omnis recta cognitio Dei ab oboedientia nascitur* (all true knowledge of God comes from obedience). The Argentinian theologian José Míguez Bonino doubtless had this sentence from Calvin in mind when he wrote: 'Obedience is not a *consequence* of our knowledge of God, just as it is not a pre-condition for it: obedience is implied in our knowledge of God. Or, to put it more bluntly: obedience *is* our knowledge of God.' This makes it clear why the Final Declaration of Dar-es-Salaam speaks of commitment as the first act of theology.

In terms of epistemology, the consequence of this biblical-theological perspective is to cast doubts on an epistemology which evades the connection that is always present between ways of thinking and ways of living, between theory and practice. The standpoint of the theologian cannot be an Archimedean point outside historical reality. Any thought, whether it recognizes that or not, stands in a context of action and is thus 'situated' and limited. The questions which people ask about God are closely connected with their view of the world, but the world of the person without possessions is different from that of the person with possessions. The slave owner and the slave may live on the same plantation, but they inhabit different worlds; their conceptions of reality and of God differ. Their hermeneutical position is conditioned by their social position. The difference is that the slave owner is the master of the slave, and therefore also – to a certain degree – of his conception of reality and of 'God'. The domination consists in the fact that the slave owner fails to recognize that another picture of reality (which might threaten his own position) is possible and legitimate: his God and his world are the only possible ones! The slave owner denies the fact (in order to maintain his social position) that his conception of 'God' as the great patriarch who rules strictly but justly over the world is an extension of his image of himself as the father who rules strictly but justly on his plantation over his children, the slaves. The slave owner would rightly feel threatened by an epistemological method which was contextual and brought out this connection with the aim of making room for the different character of the slave's understanding.

Thus the epistemological insight into the situational character of thought and the connection between thought and action, 'consciousness' and 'being', is a question which leads to criticism of ideology. Liberation theology seeks to break with an academic theology which, by relegating the question of action and commitment to second place, can keep aloof from the question of its own social conditioning. The epistemological presuppositions which make this possible derive from the notion of the freedom and autonomy of the thinking subject. However, the concept which goes with this epistemology did not drop down from the skies, but is the product of modernity; in other words, it derives from a way of thinking originating in the Enlightenment and handed down by the bourgeoisie. Liberation theologians make a connection between this concept of freedom, which reflects bourgeois experience, and an urge for expansion which claims that there is no room for experience or thought which goes beyond the subjectivity of the believer. Where theological method is based on the subjective experience and thought of the believer, and where since Schleiermacher this believer has been none other than modern, i.e. bourgeois man, theology could *de facto* become a closed argument which, while being thought to be universal, passed over the experience and thought of people living on the underside of the bourgeois success story.

Underlying this criticism of the domination of bourgeois subjectivity is an important agreement with the philosophy of Louis Althusser, from whom the term 'epistemological break' has been adopted. This term really derives from Gaston Bachelard (1884-1962), who in his epistemology argued that any science presupposes a break (*rupture*) with non-scientific knowledge; Bachelard makes a sharp distinction between *connaissance commune* and *connaissance scientifique*. Althusser in turn speaks of an epistemological caesura (*coupure*) which forms the line of demarcation between ideology and science; a model of such a caesura is Galileo's Copernican shift, or Freud's discovery of the unconscious. Althusser, however, was principally concerned with the epistemological caesura which in principle makes the scientific discipline of history possible at all; according to Althusser, the discovery of the 'continent history' and historical materialism as the method of mapping this continent are the result of a caesura which took place in the thinking of Marx about 1845: before 1845 Marx was still under the spell of the 'theoretical humanism' of Feuerbach, for whom man is the centre of history; after 1845 Marx rejects this anthropocentric philosophy of history and no longer begins with man as history maker, but with the complex of economic, political and ideological relationships; in other words with history as a structure without a subject.

However, the adoption of the term 'epistemological break' does not mean that liberation theologians take over Althusser's interpretation of Marx, much less that they identify with his theoretical position within Marxism. For example, for the Brazilian theologian Clodovis Boff, in Althusser the intellectual still has far too much the monopoly of real, legitimate knowledge. Underlying this criticism is a contrast between Althusser's efforts to restore Marxism as a science – he makes a sharp distinction between Marxist theory and the economic, political and ideological developments of the workers' movement and populist tendencies in Latin-American liberation theology, in which 'the wisdom of the people' takes on the function of mediating salvation.

Liberation theology is liberation of that theology which supposes itself to be universalist and as such passes over the diversity of situations and human needs, social tensions and conflicts, and the causes of poverty and wretchedness. It disparages the old association of this pseudo-universality with the dominant cultures, social classes and races. The epistemological break is the condition for a new form of universality which makes room for these experiences of faith and reflections on faith which are excluded by the dominant traditions of theology and teaching authority.

Therefore any form of liberation theology is also always the articulation of a history and tradition which has been brushed aside and suppressed: black theology in the United States derives from the tradition of the black 'invisible church' in the period of slavery about which our church histories usually tell us nothing, but in which we have the tradition of a unique experience of faith, the 'black experience'; Latin-American, African and Asian theologians are, each in his or her own context, in search of liberating elements in the feasts and narratives, the rites and customs of the peoples with whom they live and struggle; feminist theologians in turn try to find traces of the religious experience of women in history, however difficult that may often prove because of the lack of sources.

I spoke earlier of a new form of universality. However, the question is whether we can really continue to speak of universality if we are dealing with a black theology in which God is black, an Indian theology in which God is imagined as being red, and a feminist theology which rejects patriarchalist thinking.

The articulation of suppressed traditions of faith raises very sharply an old problem: the unity and continuity of the Christian tradition. Can the hidden experiences and reflections of faith investigated and brought to light by the different forms of liberation theology be subsumed under the same heading as these dominant Christian traditions which in our time ignore in sovereign fashion the experiences 'from the underside of history' (Gutiérrez)? Is there any question here of 'unity in difference' and of 'pluriformity', those ideas of which some ecumenical theologians are so fond? Did the cross on the banners of the *conquistadores* represent the same Christ as the Christ whom Bartolomé de Las Casas recognized in the face of the Indian? When the slave owner and the slave sang 'Amazing Grace', were they singing the same hymn? When Vorster's and Botha's omnipotent South African Broederbond opens its meetings with prayer, are they praying to the same God as the one in whom the black theologian Allan Boesak and his colleagues of the Broederkring put their trust in the struggle against apartheid?

In this context, what is the significance of the basic formula of the World Council of Churches which was accepted at New Delhi in 1961: 'The World Council of Churches is a fellowship of churches which confess the Lord Jesus Christ as God and Saviour, according to the scriptures, and therefore seek to fulfil together their common calling to the glory of the one God, Father, Son and Holy Spirit'? Is this formula the common denominator which binds churches and groups of Christians together regardless of all their confessional and social differences? Or is it a scandal to the one and only name to talk in this way? Are we forbidden, by virtue of the incarnation of the Word, to detach the rule of doctrine from the rule of life and to abstract formulas of belief from specific life-styles?

If this last is the case, then in all seriousness we must note that there is no such thing as *the* Christian tradition. In historical and empirical terms there is no demonstrable continuity of word and action in the history of Christianity. As far as the Christian tradition is concerned, it is in fact simply the arena for conflicting readings of the biblical story, interwoven in a complex way with social contrasts and conflicts, one opposed to the others – and neither academic theology nor the church's authority is impartial here!

> It would be a mistake to think that there was ever one Christian tradition. Even earliest Christianity was aware of a difference in traditions, which were often in tension with one another. In the New Testament we find clear traces of this (see, for example, Gal.2.11ff.). The continuity of tradition was already felt to be a problem in the history of the early church. The second century saw the rise of the idea of apostolic succession, the starting point for which was that the apostles appointed bishops every-

where who in turn consecrated their successors, so that the truth of Christian faith and of church doctrine was handed on in an unbroken sequence from the time of the apostles. From 325, ecumenical councils were occasionally held by the emperor in which the limits of Christian truth and tradition were laid down in dogmatic formulas: beyond these limits lay heresy. However, the beginning of the fourth century at the same time represented a break in church history: in 313 Constantine the Great declared Christianity to be a *religio licita*, an approved religion, and from that time on it functioned as the religion of ruling powers. Since this alliance between church and state, which was not in fact without its tensions, down the course of history groups and movements have been condemned as heretics and have suffered bloody persecutions although, seen from the perspective of a 'church of the poor', they in fact represented the true church.

Now if the continuity and unity of the Christian tradition cannot be demonstrated in history, then the catholicity of the church is also historically very problematical. In historical and empirical terms, the unity and catholicity of the church as the body of Christ is non-existent. But in that case what does it mean when the Apostles' Creed confesses : *credo sanctam ecclesiam catholicam*?

In the first place, it means that the catholicity of the church is a matter of faith; in other words, it is something which can be accepted in faith despite the fact that it is historically invisible.

This sounds reassuring: while we *see* conflicting traditions of faith and division within the church which are difficult to understand as pluralism, *behind* this visible reality there is clearly the unity and catholicity which we lack so grievously in this earthly vale of tears. But is this Platonism – the true reality behind the visible world – in fact what the Apostles' Creed is talking about? Is the *ecclesia catholica* a reality beyond history? Or are we not barred from thinking in this way – not so much by Hebrew thought as compared with Greek, but by the reality of the incarnation?

It has rightly been argued that in fact both the catholicity of the church and definitive dogma or *the* tradition of Christian faith are eschatological entities which cannot be verified historically or empirically and therefore are hard to believe in. However, in biblical theology, eschatology is not something that begins where our history leaves off, but a reality, God's reality, which becomes manifest in this history.

The mystery of the incarnation is betrayed when the unity of Christ's body and the catholicity of Christian doctrine is sought above, alongside or behind our history. The mystery is equally surrendered when on the other hand unity and catholicity are identified with the external authority of church pronouncements.

Just as the continuity of the history of the covenant can only be discovered in (and not beyond) the discontinuity of what we call history, so the continuity of what Karl Barth calls the threefold form of the Word – the proclaimed Word, the written Word and the revealed Word – can only be found in the discontinuity of the breaks and conflicts in history (the history of the church). However, a prophetic perspective, the perspective of a visionary, is needed to perceive this continuity and unity.

In an article on the conception of history in Old Testament prophecy (1960), Hans Walter Wolff describes the history of the covenant as a history with the structure of dialogue in which the freedom of the partners remains unaffected. Because of this last feature, 'the continuity in the specific course of history can be concealed by acute discontinuity; only through the prophetic word of disclosure does it again become visible.'

The continuity of the history of the covenant is ultimately the only assurance and guarantee of the continuity of the Christian tradition. However, no matter how universal this history is, no matter how it is intended for all human beings, it cannot be seen neutrally in terms of what happens among and between human beings: 'Truly, I say to you, that inasmuch as you have done this to one of the least of these, my brothers, you have done it to me' (Matt.25.40). In respect of what we usually call history – the history of development, progress and social success – this history acts as an anti-history. But, just as the reality of catastrophe, absolute discontinuity, is concealed beneath the apparent continuity of history – one need only think of Auschwitz – so the mystery of the incarnation points towards the mystery that the continuity of the history of the covenant can only be seen on the other side of our usual history, among the 'broken-hearted', the 'prisoners' and the 'poor' (Luke 4.16-21) – not because they have particular psychological capacities, but because they now make up the elect.

(c) Western European reactions

All the methodological and hermeneutical considerations about contextuality, the primacy of praxis and the epistemological break which we have considered above are closely connected with the concept from which this way of doing theology takes its name, liberation.

The theology of liberation challenges a privatized conception of salvation, where redemption is exclusively connected with the relationship of the individual to God. Messianic liberation embraces the whole of life. Even where this theology describes itself as 'theology of captivity' – because the oppressive reality of everyday life does away with all illusions – in the last resort it is joyful, optimistic reflection, since the promise of a new heaven and a new earth where righteousness dwells forms the horizon of this history. This happy, intense hope, despite the tears of yesterday and today, is not a private perspective on life, but reflects the ecstatic spirituality of black liturgy or the celebration of the eucharist in a basic community in Brazil or Central America. Liberation is the prospect in the specific everyday struggle of the poor for their elementary rights to life – to this degree the concept of liberation is always set in a specific historical context; at the same time it is the deep awareness that the liberation of classes, races or groups can never be complete without the liberation of *all* people – and this last insight makes liberation an eschatological reality. Therefore liberation theology operates in the field of tension between history and eschatology, particularity and universality. History and eschatology do not merge, far less can they be played off, one against the other. The vital dialectical tension between the two is the hallmark and the touchstone of authentic liberation theology, in whatever context.

Of course this last point does not mean that the way in which individual liberation theologians have thought through and expressed this tension stands above all criticism. However, it does mean that two kinds of reactions which one still comes across in this connection fall short of the mark.

The first reaction is that liberation theology, in an intrinsically justified protest against a timeless and privatized proclamation of the gospel, has now gone to the other extreme by allowing the gospel to be swallowed up in social action. This reaction overlooks the fact that the eschatological expectation which is never satisfied by any political programme is itself the breeding ground for subversive social action. It is far too simple to suppose that liberation theology first makes a political choice which is subsequently legitimated by a 'one-sided' reading of the Bible. This reaction remains sterile and leads nowhere as long as it refuses to take seriously the questions raised by liberation theologians about contextuality and the relationship between theory and praxis.

A second common reaction sees liberation theology in the context of the Third World as a more or less legitimate variant of the Western theological tradition(s), a variant which can be valid for purely social and psychological reasons (for example to get rid of frustrations and feelings of inferiority) but which is (*a*) determined by its situation and is therefore less relevant to us and (*b*) still has to prove its scientific content. What this reaction fails to note is that it is the creative tension between particularity and universality which makes liberation theology an ecumenical theology that ultimately has the whole world as its horizon. Its polemical attitude towards dominant theological traditions does not change this in any way: on the contrary, it is this critical attitude which puts it within the ambit of the 'appeal structures of the world church' (L.A.Hoedemaker).

The fact that this and similar reactions to liberation theology fall short of the mark does not mean that there is no real conflict about the relationship of particularity to universality, history to eschatology, between Western European theology and Third-World theology. The experiences with the 'German Christians' in the time of National Socialism and the significance of the Barmen theses developed in this situation, in which Karl Barth and others rejected any mixture of gospel and political ideology, mean that on the basis of the so-called eschatological proviso most European theologians firmly maintain the qualitative difference between eschatology and history, between God's revolution and our revolutions. But what does it mean to play off this eschatological proviso against the struggle of the poor for a worthwhile human existence? Does it mean that the poor must be content with their lot because in this history any revolution turns into its opposite and the oppressed of today become the oppressors of tomorrow? The relationship between eschatology and history is perhaps *the* central problem in the confrontation between dominant theological traditions and forms of liberation theology. However, if this relationship is reduced to an abstract set of theological problems without proper discussion of the methodological and hermeneutical questions raised by the liberation theologians, then the debate will be especially barren.

It is obvious that liberation theology should provoke resistance in our context, given its polemical character, and that in itself is no occasion for deep discontent. It is more worrying that in some circles liberation theology is receiving an uncritical welcome which hardly does its cause any good. Having already been mistreated so often in history, the poor are now being used to rescue Western Christians from their crisis of identity – which seems to be all the more convenient the further away these poor are – in the Philippines or in El Salvador. For in our context it is by no means clear what is meant by 'church of the poor', 'liberation', 'solidarity'. Here the language of liberation theology is taken over but its perspective is destroyed.

The rejection and negation of liberation theology on the one hand and the uncritical welcome to it on the other do, however, have one thing in common: both focus on the real challenge of liberation theology, which lies in its otherness. One could say that liberation theology confronts bourgeois religion with the challenge of otherness (E.Levinas), the otherness of the other (Other). Annexation and negation are the two ways of avoiding this challenge. The particularity of any form of liberation theology does not allow it to be transposed uncritically to other situations; equally, the universal tendency of this theology, in the last instance based on the oneness and uniqueness of the Name (Deut.6.4), does not allow it to be negated any longer. To pass between this Scylla and Charybdis we have to take the questions and experiences from another context so seriously that they sharpen our attention to what is happening in our own context, so that 'the other' is really seen here, and theology becomes possible as a critical reflection on a praxis of liberation.

3

Black Theology

The first form of theology which we shall be looking at in more detail is black theology. The struggle against racism, as carried on by black people in the United States, South Africa and elsewhere, forms the historical and social context of this question. Its basic question is, what is the gospel of Jesus Christ for people who are oppressed because of 'racial' characteristics?

The great Afro-American leader W.E.B. du Bois prophesied in 1903 that the problem of the twentieth century would be the problem of the colour line. Now that we are almost at the end of the twentieth century, we have to confirm that racism has indeed been one of the basic forms of oppression – and the end of the struggle over race is far from being in sight. However, the remarkable thing (and at the same time this is part of the problem) is that modern humane and social sciences constantly seem to underestimate racism as a system of oppression. In bourgeois societies, people are inclined to concentrate on the attitude and the mentality of individuals and groups in society and to lose sight of the fact that racism is above all a problem of the complex relationship of economic, political and ideological power struc-tures. Marxists, who regard the class struggle as the motive power of history, have difficulty in seeing racism as more than a concomitant of the class struggle. However, the race struggle has a specific dynamic of its own, which cannot be reduced to other forms of domination and exploitation. In practice racism seems to be a many-headed monster, which keeps raising a head where people do not expect it. The demonic power of this monster lies not least in the impossibility of analysing it adequately.

Still, if we are to gain access to phenomena like black theology

or the Rastafarian movement, we need to have some understanding of what racism is and its consequences in human hearts
and human social structures. So before discussing black theology
in this chapter, we shall first, however summarily, investigate this
extremely complex and delicate question.

(*a*) Racism and slavery

The definition of a social phenomenon like racism is as necessary
as it is dangerous. The danger lurks in the fact that definition is
never a neutral, innocent occupation. Lewis Carroll showed that
brilliantly:

> 'When I use a word,' Humpty Dumpty said in a rather scornful
> tone, 'it means just what I choose it to mean – neither more nor
> less.' 'The question is,' said Alice, 'whether you can make words
> mean so many different things.' 'The question is,' said Humpty
> Dumpty, 'which is to be master – that's all.'

All down history, defining, classifying and recording has mainly
been the privilege of dominant élites, and it seems constantly to
be bound up with particular effects of power – it is also to be
found precisely where people refer to social objectivity and
autonomy. Nowhere is that expressed more blatantly in the
contemporary world situation, as far as racism is concerned, than
in the South African system of apartheid, where people are defined
as, i.e. reduced to, being 'black', 'coloured', 'Indian', where
specific 'racial' characteristics are attributed to these categories
to explain and justify their inferior social status, and where such
a classification puts the dominant white élite in the position of
being able to carry out a sophisticated policy of divide and
conquer.

However, the danger of reduction is enormous even where
theorizing about 'the racial question' is done by opponents of
radical oppression – theorizing which still seems to be mostly an
activity for whites. There is a stubborn refusal to see the hard core
of racism as the ideological organization of exploitation and
dependence. So it is still quite common today to find racism
defined in terms of attitude, prejudice and behaviour. However
true it may also be that racial oppression is indissolubly bound
up with prejudices, discriminatory behaviour and ethnocentrism,

in such definitions *the material basis of racism* is ignored: racism is reduced to something which takes place inside human heads, and the implicit presupposition here is that a change of attitude which will put an end to racial oppression can be brought about by dialogue, by an ethical appeal for a change of mentality. A similar difficulty appears where racism is described as dogma (Ruth Benedict), as belief-systems (William J.Wilson) or as a set of beliefs, as happens in the well-known study *Race and Racism* by Pierre L. van den Berghe:

> Racism is any set of beliefs that organic, genetically transmitted differences (whether real or imagined) between human groups are intrinsically associated with the presence or the absence of certain socially relevant abilities or characteristics.

Here, too, the hard core – the power factor – is chopped out of the intrinsically ingenious definition. The main accent in such an approach lies unavoidably and unchangeably on the thought or action of (groups of) individual subjects which are thought to be autonomous, and something of this kind is always a dangerous underestimation of the way in which racism is embedded in the economic, political-juridical and ideological structures of society, and deeply rooted in the collective unconsciousness associated with them. Illustrative of the language of such thinking about racism is the fact that when in 1968 the World Council of Churches took the decision in principle to embark on a programme of action to combat racism (the PCR), it did so on the basis of a definition, still completely bound up with ideas about dialogue and moral appeal which in the meantime has proved ineffective. The 1968 World Council Assembly defined racism as follows:

> By racism we mean ethnocentric *pride* in one's own racial group preference for the distinctive characteristics of that group; belief that these characteristic are fundamentally biological in nature and are thus transmitted to succeeding generations; strong negative feelings towards other groups who do not share these characteristics coupled with the thrust to discriminate against and exclude the outgroup from full participation in the life of the community.

Without doubt racism is also all these things: ethnocentric arrogance and discrimination against the outgroup are certainly important aspects of racial oppression. However, the experiences of the PCR, especially in South Africa, make it clear that racism is above all a system of oppression.

To express this last fact, the PCR adopts a term which crops up for the first time in Stokely Carmichael and Charles V. Hamilton's *Black Power*, published in 1967: institutional racism. Carmichael and Hamilton point out that racism is both open and concealed, and that it takes on two closely related aspects: individual whites acting against individual blacks, and actions of the total white community against the black community. The authors call the first form 'individual racism' and the second 'institutional racism'. 'When a black family moves into a home in a white neighbourhood and is stoned, burned or routed out, they are victims of an overt act of individual racism which many people will condemn – at least in words. But it is institutional racism that keeps black people locked in dilapidated slum tenements, subject to the daily prey of exploitative slumlords, merchants, loan sharks and discriminatory real estate agents. The society either pretends it does not know of this latter situation, or is in fact incapable of doing anything meaningful about it.'

The discovery of institutional racism is an important advance. However, Carmichael's and Hamilton's theory also raises questions: What is the connection between individual and institutional racism? Is individual racism always open?, and so on. The insights of both authors take on their own emphasis when we see them against the background of the struggle for equal civil rights in the United States and the rise of Black Power. Their study is a direct, militant intervention in the racial struggle of the 1960s, and as such is partisan and contextual. This last statement, however, raises an important question: Is not any social theory already *a priori* 'situated', in other words limited by time and place? Is a general theory and description of racism really possible?

The consultation on 'Racism in the 1980s' held by the PCR in Noordwijkerhout, Holland, in June 1980, with good reason resolved for the moment not to give a general definition. On the basis of their experience in previous years there was a plea for a contextual approach, in which the specific form in which racism manifested itself was constantly investigated in specific situations. The combatting of racism had to be grounded in contextually based definitions and theories, without forgetting that the widest context in which racism manifests itself today is the international capitalist system.

However, at the consultation in Noordwijkerhout, at the same time it became clear to what danger such an approach was exposed. Virtually all the world problems today were discussed – the North-South relationship, ecology, the arms race, and so on – without it always becoming clear precisely what the racist element was in them. In this way concepts were blurred: the word racism began to mean so much that it ended up meaning nothing.

Consequently it is important to go on looking for a working definition of racism which is sufficiently clear to distinguish the historical reality of the race struggle from other basic forms of social struggle including those relating to class and sex. I suggest the following definition:

> Racism is the specific ideology which organizes and regulates the exploitation and dependence of a particular 'race' (group, people) on the basis of the supposed cultural and/or biological inferiority of this 'race', and in this way perpetuates and deepens already existing differences of power.

In this definition the word race is put in inverted commas in order to show that in this context the term is part of the problem: historically, the division of humanity on the basis of morphological and physiological characteristics with the aim of being able to derive racial differences and psychological properties from this division and to use it as a basis for positing the superiority of one race over another, is closely connected with the rise of Western/white racism. We use the term ideology here – following Gramsci and Althusser – to denote a way of thinking about reality which is not limited to what goes on in human heads but leads a material existence; it finds expression in the total social reality in which we are involved as individuals – in institutions like churches, schools and law courts, and also in architecture and music. As such it precedes the individual and forms his or her world, determining what is taken for granted within that world. When we talk of racism as ideology, we recognize that the real danger of this historical and social phenomenon lies in the natural and obvious way in which it presents itself and forces itself on us – not just on the rulers but also on those whom they oppress, since their oppression consists precisely in the fact that they believe what the dominant ideology says about them (internalization). 'Racism is natural, antiracism is not' (Albert Memmi).

Western/white racism, as it has eaten into our culture, is a historical phenomenon; in other words, the natural and obvious way in which it manifests itself has not always been natural and obvious. Racism as ideology has come to life in a particular historical constellation, bearing out the truth of what is said by the American historian Eugene D. Genovese, following Gramsci: 'Once an ideology arises it profoundly alters the material reality and in fact become a partially autonomous feature of that reality.' However much racism may also be the consequence of economic developments and relationships, once it has arisen, at least partially it takes on an autonomous existence which in turn has a profound influence on the level of economic and political life.

Leaving aside the question of the presence of racism at other times and in other, distant cultures (and we can similarly leave aside the complicated question of the relationship between anti-semitism and white racism), we can say that the historical context of racism, which still exists in our time and in our culture, was formed by the development of bourgeois capitalist society and the Western colonial expansion which went with it. The rise of the Atlantic slave trade and black slavery in the New World was of crucial significance. Comparative historical studies of slavery in Latin America, North America and the Caribbean sphere produce an extremely complicated picture which cannot be summarized in a few sentences. The position of blacks, both slave and free, was not the same everywhere, however deplorable the situation may have been generally. For example, racial mixing was usual in a country like Brazil, while in the British colonies of North America it was strongly disapproved of and sometimes forbidden by law. However, we must allow ourselves one generalization: the most powerful forms of racial oppression arose and still arise in areas where a Puritan Calvinistic ethic prevails – one might think of the period of segregation in the southern states of the USA and apartheid in South Africa.

In his book *Capitalism and Slavery*, published in 1944, which was rediscovered in the 1960s, Eric Williams, later the premier of Trinidad and Tobago, defended the viewpoint that the origin of black slavery is not based on racial but on economic causes, just as further economic development at a later stage made slavery an anachronism. Whereas in the mercantile period with its trade monopolies slavery was extremely profitable, in later industrial capitalism there was in fact as little room for slavery as there was for monopolies. That in trade over the Atlantic triangle Dutch, English and French ships transported black slaves from West Africa to the New World was in the first instance not the result of racism; in fact the Africans were the only ones who had the physical strength to survive slave work. In the New World the Indian had been the first slave, but this experiment proved a great failure. After that the poor white took his place: the overseas trade began with white slaves! However, compared with the Indian and the white man, the black man made up a far superior work force. In Williams' view racism is not a cause but a consequence of black slavery. The decisive factor was not the colour of the slave-worker's skin but the cheapness of his labour. Slavery was introduced for economic, not racial motives. Racism is no more than the subsequent rationalization of black slavery as a form of economic exploitation.

Eric Williams is not alone in his view. And if racism must indeed be described as organized oppression and does not just coincide with prejudice, ethnocentrism and so on, then his view is more capable of being defended than the current theory in which slavery is regarded as a consequence of the prior existence of racism in Western and especially Anglo-Saxon culture. However, the question remains how the inhuman slave trade and slavery could be accepted so easily, and indeed specifically, by those who were filled with the highest humanitarian ideals. Williams gives no answer to this question. The shortcoming in his approach lies in the excessive stress on economics at the expense of ideology, and the underestimation of the prejudice against black Africa which was already deep-seated in Western culture.

In his study *White over Black* (1968), Winthrop D. Jordan has shown that the way in which the British colonists pictured their new world was steeped in the contrast between white and black: they saw America as a land of the whites, and freedom meant freedom for whites; African heathen in fact had no place in this Christian dream-world of white freedom and equality, and they could only be tolerated as aliens in the land to which they had been brought against their will to be exploited as slaves.

According to Jordan, this tendency to define the distinctive identity of whites by contrasting them with blacks did not arise on American soil, but was brought from England. From the first moment that English seafarers and traders came into contact with black Africans, the most fantastic stories went the rounds about their lust and their affinity to ape-men, which had just been discovered: blackness was associated with paganism, with savagery, lust and bestiality. A black skin was associated with the old genealogical myth that the Africans were the descendants of Ham; Shem, Ham and Japheth were the sons of Noah, but in contrast to his brothers Ham was cursed by his father and his descendants were doomed to slavery (cf.Gen.9.25ff.). The black skin of Africans and what the English felt to be their repugnant appearance was seen as a divine punishment for their abiding transgression of all sexual norms.

Jordan seeks the explanation for the ease with which the stories and fables about Africa were accepted as true in a theory of projection: in the seventeenth century, with its rapid social changes, the English saw in others what they could not accept as being present in themselves. Unexpressed sexual feelings were projected on to black Africans, who to British society were already beginning to embody what they themselves were compelled to denounce and reject as abnormal and deviant behaviour.

We can leave on one side here the question how far Jordan's theory needs supplementing or correcting. The important thing is that shortly before the introduction of slavery there was clearly a conglomerate of prejudices and myths which made this human practice socially acceptable.

During the period of systems of slavery in North America, Latin America and the Caribbean there was then a gradual transition from ethnocentricity, prejudice and the like to racism as a specific form of organized oppression; despite all the similarities, this took on different contours depending on the area. The more opposition to this slavery and the fear of slave rebellions increased, the more powerfully this racist ideology developed into a coherent practice which found expression in the numerous slave codes, in the caste restrictions for both slaves and free blacks, and in the humiliating rites and customs of the plantations which were repeated every day. Especially in the old south of the United States, this racism developed into a unique conceptualization of reality which has been described by Eugene D. Genovese and other historians as paternalism: in a stubborn attempt to overcome the fundamental contradiction in the system – which lies in the fact that slaves are human beings and not things, the cattle and the property that they are supposed to be – the planter identifies himself with the strict yet just patriarchal figure who watches over his immature children.

However, we should not lose sight of the fact that the racialist theories in Europe and North America which provided 'scientific' support for the superiority of the white races only enjoyed great popularity when the development of industrial capitalism and the expansion of the world market had made slavery a hopeless anachronism. It is no coincidence that the rise of social Darwinism coincides historically with the period of imperialism which begins about 1870; the idea of the survival of the fittest goes remarkably well with the pitiless colonial wars of conquest and the principle of free competition. In practice it was interpreted as the law of the strongest and served as a scientific cloak for imperialist aggression.

The combination of belief in progress with both a hierarchical division of races and a biological determinism served as a legitimation for the rule and the expansionist policies of the 'Herrenvolk democracies' (Pierre L. van den Berghe). For someone like Herbert Spencer, the first to formulate the terms 'survival of the fittest' and 'struggle for life', it went without saying that the progress of humanity had to take place under the leadership of the white race, and for Francis Galton, the founder of eugenics and a nephew of Darwin, the average level of the black race was 'two stages' lower than that of the white race, and that of the Australian aborigines 'three stages lower'.

The popularity of biological and anthropological theories among political and military authorities does not, however, disguise the unmistakeable fact that the extreme forms of racial hatred which appear at the end of the nineteenth century have their basis in the anxieties of the petty-bourgeois. The antisemitism which appeared on a massive scale in countries like Germany and France is particularly connected with the small independent businessmen and wage-earners who felt on the one hand the threat to their existence from the high flight of bank and industrial capital and the periodic recurrence of economic crises, and on the other hand the hot breath of the rising socialist workers' movement on their necks. In the south of the United States it was similarly the insignificant white man who, anxious about losing his all-too-insecure position on the labour market to the black slave who had been freed in the meantime, formed an alliance with the leading élite to exclude the black population from white society; in all the southern states a rigid segregation, carried to absurd extremes, was made law, and this was to continue down to the 1960s.

Moreover, it would be wrong to think that the 'scientific' support for the theory of the superiority of the white race is an invention of the nineteenth century. The racial theorists of this period were able to build on the work of their predecessors from the eighteenth century, the century of the Enlightenment and the bourgeois revolution. As far as racism is concerned, the Enlightenment shows a Janus-like head: on one side it expresses freedom and tolerance, and on the other some of its most important champions laid the foundations for the subsequent 'scientific' racism of De Gobineau and Houston Stewart Chamberlain.

No one embodies this contradiction better than Voltaire, the enigmatic patriarch of Ferney. In his *Essai sur les moeurs et l'esprit des nations*, this critical rationalist fulminates against slavery, but at the same time, in a considerably less rational vein, he writes: 'Only a blind man could doubt the fact that whites, Negroes and albinos (...) belong to completely different races'; he then goes on to describe the Negro as bestial.

The Enlightenment is also ambivalent in its attitude towards slavery: on the one hand its conceptions and ideals had a powerful influence on the struggle for the abolition of the slave trade and slavery; on the other it had a tendency to defend slavery on the basis of utility, ethical relativism or the inferiority of the black race. Condorcet represents true universalism when in his lettter to the Negro slaves he writes: 'Although I am not the same colour as you, I have always regarded you as my brothers. Nature created you for the possession of the same spirit, the same reason and the same virtues as the whites.' But over against Condorcet, Montesquieu or Condillac we have the view of famous natural scientists like Buffon and Linnaeus; for Buffon, Negroes were a degenerate race, and his Swedish colleague described the Negro, the *Afer niger*, as wily, idle and negligent, governed by the arbitrary will of his master, the white European, the *Europaeus albus*, who by contrast was clever, resourceful, and governed by laws.

What is the explanation of this deep ambivalence towards slavery and towards people with skins of a different colour? This question can only be answered if we recognize in the Janus head of the Enlightenment the features of the bourgeois (then still a revolutionary) who on the one hand was driven by the vision of humanity in freedom, equality and brotherhood, but on the other hand put freedom into practice in a way which meant oppression and captivity for others.

In the last resort this flagrant contradiction between the struggle for universal human happiness and the practice of exploitation and discrimination could only be solved by saying that the oppressed groups and classes were not truly human: humanity is then in fact represented only by the white race. No less a figure than David Hume wrote in 1754: 'I am apt to suspect the Negroes, and in general all the other species of men (for there are four or five different kinds) to be naturally inferior to the whites. There never was a civilized nation with any other complexion than white, nor even any individual eminent either in action or speculation.'

If the Enlightenment is ambivalent towards slavery and latent racism, the same is true, if possible to an even greater degree, of Christianity. We need not repeat here what was said in the first chapter about mission and colonial expansion, divine election and ethnocentrism. The attitude of Christianity towards slavery has been well typified by the historian David Brion Davis as that of 'compensating dualisms': 'Slavery was contrary to the ideal realm of nature, but was a necessary part of the world of sin; the bondsman was inwardly free and spiritually equal to his master, but in things external he was a mere chattel; Christians were brothers, whether slave or free, but pagans deserved in some sense to be slaves.'

This Christian dualism in respect of slavery in the New World could look back on a long tradition. It was not essentially different from the attitude which the church of the first centuries had towards ancient slavery. The church fathers left slavery untouched as the foundation of Graeco-Roman society. In this respect we can note a striking difference between the early church and the Jewish synagogue. Of course the Jewish people, too, did not really do away with slavery, but the result of the constant re-telling of the story of the liberation from the slavery of Egypt meant that there was a good deal of opposition in the Torah to slavery as a means of exploitation (cf. the institution of the year of Jubilee in Lev.25.40-42; also Ex.21.2-11; Deut.23.15); K.H.Kroon points out: 'Of course this Jewish belief in liberation proved extremely attractive above all to slaves of non-Jewish descent, who observed that every Jewish ecclesia was obliged to redeem its members who had become slaves and in fact actually did so. The belief was singularly unattractive to the Roman establishment in particular: a Jewish slave did not work on one day of the week, and that also applied to a non-Jewish slave who had become a full member of the Jewish community.'

In the early church, however, the fact that both the master and the slave were baptized in the name of Christ and thus entered into a relationship of brotherly *agape* (love) in the Christian community had no consequence for their other social relationships and for existing circumstances in society. All too soon the dualism of body and soul, internal and external, eternal and temporal, to be found in Hellenistic culture, took over Christian teaching and life-style. The freedom of the children of God was understood as an inner, spiritual freedom which left existing social circumstances untouched. In the pattern of salvation history which the church father Augustine supported in his weak moments, people were equal before the Fall, but the universality of sin after the Fall necessitated the authority of one person over another. The letter of the apostle Paul to Philemon about the runaway slave Onesimus was not interpreted by the church fathers as a 'subversive letter' (K.H.Kroon), but more as an encouragement to both master and slave to remain true to their social positions, since the existing differences were the will of God. This interpretation was not just intended to reassure the political authorities that Christianity was not concerned to bring about social change; certainly theologians like Theodore of Mopsuestia (died 428) used it as a polemical weapon against the radical monasticism of the followers of Eustathius of Sebaste and the Circumcelliones in North Africa, who rejected both marriage and slavery and private possessions.

The rediscovery of Christian freedom in the Reformation did

not bring about any essential change in this state of affairs. Only the radical wing of the Reformation really sought to subvert existing conditions. However, like the early church fathers, Luther used the letter to Philemon to refute chiliastic conceptions. He maintained against Thomas Müntzer and the fanatics that the apostle Paul in no way wanted to do away with slavery, and expressly gave Philemon the right to possess his slave. When in 1525 the peasants in Swabia based their freedom from slavery on the fact that Christ had freed all men, Luther rejected this concept of freedom as 'utterly fleshly' and in conflict with scripture.

However, in the Christian tradition, alongside this spiritualistic conception of liberty, another motive determined relationships towards slavery. From earliest times sin was seen as slavery: 'anyone who sins is a slave of sin' (John 8.34; cf. Rom.6.15-23); and for someone like Augustine it is better to be another man's slave than the slave of one's own libido.

This view can be stood on its head: if sin is slavery, then slavery as a form of social organization is sin, and Augustine does in fact see slavery as a consequence of sin, a fate that befalls human beings because of the divine judgment, which is never unjust, and which allots different punishments to men and women depending on the crimes that they have committed (*De civitate Dei* XIX, 15).

This causal connection between sin, slavery and divine judgment proved disastrous, especially in Anglo-Saxon and Dutch Calvinism. If we remember how the cursing of Ham was connected with black Africa and how blackness was associated with lust (libido) and bestiality, then it becomes clear why so many Christians and theologians saw the Africans as a doomed race and had no difficulty in reconciling their slavery with God's righteousness and predetermined will.

When in the seventeenth century churches were already putting pressure on the black slave trade and slavery – though this was not often the case – they were exclusively concerned with the question whether black slaves could be baptized and receive religious instruction. Many people rejected both the baptism of slaves and their religious instruction on the grounds that (*a*) black slaves could not be regarded as human beings and (*b*) religious instruction could be a source of rebellion and therefore was in conflict with the interest of the planters, who had paid hard cash for their slaves. The institution of slavery as such was not attacked by the churches. Even the Society of Friends (the Quakers) accepted it as normal, and many members themselves had slaves or had invested in the slave trade; indeed in 1700 the Pennsylvania Assembly, dominated by Quakers, could accept one of the strictest northern slave codes, which among other features rejected the legalization of the marriage of slaves and prescribed castration as a punishment for any black man who violated a white woman.

However, already in the seventeenth century there were Quakers who showed the other face of Christianity and raised their voices – as individuals – against the inhuman system of slavery. In Pennsylvania in 1688 a number of Germantown Quakers protested against slavery on the basis of the Golden Rule (Matt.7.12; Luke 6.31), and so in their own way did William Edmundson and George Keith; the description which Keith gives in his pamphlet of the mission of Christ in the world is particularly striking: it is 'to ease and delight the Oppressed and Distressed, and bring them into Liberty both inward and outward'.

The real breakthrough among the Quakers, however, took place in 1753 when John Woolman published his *Some Considerations on the Keeping of Negroes*, written about seven years earlier, and in 1758 the Annual Assembly in Philadelphia resolved to excommunicate anyone who bought or sold a slave. This decision was the direct result of the process of deep reflection and purification to which the Society of Friends felt itself called after its rejection of Pennsylvania's involvement in the cruelties of the seven-year war, the 'French and Indian War'. Still, however much from then on the Quakers were increasingly among the vanguard in the struggle for the abolition of slavery, it should not be forgotten that they were primarily concerned with religious purity in their own circles. They were most deeply concerned with this purity and not with the fate of the black slave; although they made provision for religious instruction for blacks, until 1796 they were not prepared to accept them into their own congregations, and for a long time after that, membership by black people was certainly not encouraged. Moreover, it is striking to what extent the philosophers of the Enlightenement recognized their ideals in these capitalist, well-to-do apostles of tolerance: the inner light of the Spirit among the Quakers shows a marked affinity to the light of reason among the *philosophes* and it says much for the way in which the Quaker community in Pennsylvania was regarded as a model when we see the Quaker held up in the influential work by Abbé Raynal, *Histoire philosophique et politique des établissements et du commerce européens dans les deux Indes* as the virtuous, thrifty, orderly bearer of a great future. So we must conclude that where for the first time in history – apart from heretical, chiliastic movements – Christianity showed another face to slaves, its features had a striking likeness to those of the Enlightenment.

To begin with, it seemed that the Methodists would follow the example of the Quakers. John Wesley's *Thoughts upon Slavery* (1774) spoke out clearly, and also the leaders of American Methodism, Francis Asbury and Thomas Coke, were also opponents of slavery. In 1780 an assembly of seventeen preachers, held in Baltimore, resolved to free their own slaves and to instruct other Methodists to do the same. A decisive step was taken in 1784 when it was resolved to excommunicate all Methodists who had not emancipated their slaves within two years. Other evangelical groups moved in the same direction: in 1787 the Presbyterians voted for definitive abolition, and in 1789 the Baptists condemned slavery as a 'violation of natural rights and in conflict with a republican régime'.

The heightened emotions and heart-searchings and the deep struggles of conscience over the barbaric system of slavery show that the waves of evangelization which flooded America after the Great Awakening of 1739-1742 were impelled by religious forces that embraced more than simply a concern for the salvation of individual souls in a world of sin, on the point of perishing in fire and brimstone. We cannot transport ourselves to this wonderful religious world of the old South with its travelling preachers – some educated but most of them not – fanatics, prophets and the possessed, with its revivals and camp meetings lasting for days, in which the moaning and groaning about personal sinfulness and corruption were as much in the air as the ecstasy of collective conversion, and in which sexual debauchery, barking exercises, miraculous healings and equally miraculous visions followed one upon the other. However, two aspects are particularly important if we want to understand something of the attitude of Methodists, Baptists, Presbyterians and kindred groups to black slaves: 1. the deep emotional experience of personal *conversion* is all-pervasive;

2. the authenticity of this conversion can only emerge from a life of strict self-discipline and personal *sanctification*. This last feature meant that these evangelicals could not avoid the question of the relationship between religious purity and social justice any more than the Quakers could. The experience of conversion in turn made black and white equal in the sight of God; the fact that black people, too, underwent the experience of remorse, penitence and conversion and thus showed themselves open to God's grace was an unmistakeable confirmation of their humanity. 'This last matter is very important because the conversion experience, which whites believed had elevated all believers to a common level, could not be denied all its egalitarian implications for blacks, despite racial stereotypes, anxieties and fears', writes the historian Donald G.Mathews in his masterly study *Religion of the Old South*. However, despite the universal implications of evangelical belief, in white Puritan morality there remained a deep physical antipathy to blacks and to the sexual propensities attributed to them. While they were recognized as human beings, that did not change their inferiority in any way. Their place during church services was on the back bench or in the gallery.

The Methodists may have made a bold decision in 1784, but they were unable to maintain their radical stance for more than six months. The opposition of slave owners was so powerful that the decision had to be revoked. In subsequent years the slave rebellion led by Gabriel Prosser in Virginia, which took place in 1800, intensified both the white fear of rebellion and the opposition of slave owners to attempts to convert their slaves. In various states the slave codes were intensified, and new laws prohibited religious meetings of blacks. In connection with this last point we should remember that Prosser's uprising, and also the later revolts led by Denmark Vesey and Nat Turner, were of religious inspiration. The hostile mood against champions of the emancipation of slaves was abundantly expressed in the burning of Methodist anti-slavery pamphlets in Charleston in 1800. In 1816 the Methodist General Assembly conceded defeat and in 1818 the Presbyterians went a step further by branding slavery as a moral dilemma, but disowning the activities of champions of abolition as a source of social unrest.

Gradually, capitulation to the existing order increasingly displaced the egalitarian tendency inherent in the gospel. The accent came to lie on improving social conditions within the existing system by reminding both master and slave of their Christian duty as formulated in Eph.6.5-9: 'Slaves, show obedience to your masters in the flesh with fear and trembling, in simplicity of heart, as to Christ...' 'Those evangelicals who had condemned slavery found themselves defending slave conversion for making slaves "better", which was easily transported into making "better slaves"' (Albert J.Raboteau). Church leaders and travelling missionaries tried to gain the trust of slave owners by putting all the emphasis on the notion that it was better to make slaves obedient by means of the gospel than by threatening them with the whip. Thus even the mission to the plantations, which got well under way between 1830 and 1840, became above all a means of social control.

The leading theoretician of these mission activities was without doubt the Presbyterian preacher Charles Colcock Jones, nicknamed 'the apostle of the Negro slaves'. His numerous writings provide a good picture of the instruction given to slaves and the problems which arose as a result. The Revd C.C.Jones, himself a slave owner, was also the author of *A Catechism for Colored Persons*, a work which was so popular that it was even translated into Armenian and Chinese. The following quotation from the revised version of 1837 is characteristic of the religious instruction given to the slaves.

Question What command has God given to Servants, concerning obedience to their Masters?
Answer Slaves obey in all things your Masters according to the flesh, not in eye-service as men-pleasers, but in singleness of heart, fearing God.
Q What are Servants to count their Masters worthy of?
A All honor.
Q How are they to do their service of their Master?
A With good will, doing service unto the Lord and not unto men.
Q How are they to try to please their Master?
A Please them well in all things, not answering again.
Q Is it right in a Servant when commanded to be sullen and slow, and answer his Master again?
A No.

Things could also be put in a far less sophisticated way, as is evident from the catechetical dialogue between a Methodist preacher and a slave in Alabama.

Q What did God make you for?
A To make a crop.

How did the slaves themselves react to this proclamation of the gospel? Something which happened to C.C.Jones and which he himself relates is illuminating here. In 1833, while he was preaching about the letter of Paul to Philemon before a great congregation of slaves and was stressing the importance for slaves of the Christian virtues of fidelity and obedience, at the same time dwelling on Paul's condemnation of running away, half his audience got up and left the service, while the remainder who stayed showed themselves anything but well-disposed towards the preacher and his teaching. At the end there was a great uproar among them: some solemnly declared that 'there could not be such a letter in the Bible', others that they would not give much to hear this preacher again.

This story by the Revd C.C.Jones is not an isolated incident. The egalitarian implications of the proclamation of Christian faith did not escape the slaves – and in connection with the African religious heritage that the slave brought with him, it formed the basis for a distinctive and unique experience of faith. As Albert J.Raboteau has rightly pointed out, Christianity was a two-edged sword. In the hands of the slave owners and white preachers it functioned as an instrument for manipulating the existing slave society; and the God who was proclaimed by the missionaries on the plantations showed harsh, patriarchal features which suspiciously had much of the earthly master about them. This strict God was too powerful to be moved by slaves. We also find traces of this God in the songs and stories of the black slaves. But despite all the faults, excesses and ambiguities, the faith of the black men and women in the plantations in the deep South formed another world which protected them against the daily humiliations and dehumanizing cruelties, and despite everything gave them a sense of their own identity and human worth. In a world which treated them as cattle, the anonymous slaves encountered Jesus as a friend who knew their name: 'Hush! Somebody's calling my name'; who knew what they were suffering, 'Nobody knows de trouble I see, Nobody knows but Jesus'; who wiped away their tears, 'O Mary, don't you weep, don't you mourn'; and who in the darkness of the present gave hope of a future of freedom: 'O Canaan, sweet Canaan, I am bound for the land of Canaan.' Nowhere is the other, liberating face of Christianity turned towards black slavery expressed more clearly than in the faith of the black slave.

The slaves were deeply mistrustful of the way in which the white authorities interpreted the Bible. Whenever it was in any way possible, they preferred black preachers. Even learning to read the Bible was strictly forbidden to slaves. That the Bible nevertheless plays so important a role in black songs, sermons and stories, is a result of the slaves' capacity to remember what they had once heard: 'their memory is their book', a missionary rightly observed. Despite the alienating oppressive setting in which the biblical stories were put by white interpretation of them, the biblical stories spoke straight to the heart of the slaves: they recognized themselves in the situation of the Jewish people in Egypt, in the struggle between David and Goliath, in Daniel in the lions' den, in the crucified Jesus and in Mary by the tomb. These stories had meanings for the black slaves which they did not have for their white masters, not only because of the slaves' social position as outcasts but also because they came from Africa. Though it is true that the gods from Africa had not survived the forced crossing of the Atlantic ocean, their religious experience made it impossible for the black slaves to accept the dualism of body and soul, secular and sacred, now and hereafter, which was so typical of white Christianity. They found incredible the proclamation of an omnipotent Christian God who was exclusively concerned with the salvation of their eternal souls but who left untouched the daily hell in which they had to live. Gayraud S. Wilmore, a prominent representative of present-day black theology, gives pointed expression to this when he says:

> The grim determination and sanctimonious punctiliousness with which most Protestant missionaries went about the business of saving the souls of the heathen from eternal damnation was foreign to the basic nature of the slave's religious sensibilities. Reverence toward the Supreme Being was, for the slave, first of all, the joyous affirmation of his presence and protection.

Once the gods had come near, one opened himself to them with a vivaciousness and abandon that were expressed most satisfactorily in song and dance. The secular and the sacred met and embraced each other in the bodily celebration of the homologous unity of all things – the holy and the profane, the good and evil, the beautiful and dreadful. To give oneself up with shouts of triumph and 'singing feet' to this wholeness of being, to the ecstatic acquisition of one's own creaturehood, and to experience in frenzy that creatureliness taken up and possessed by the familiar God, was to imbibe the most restorative medicine available to the soul.

When we note that for the black slaves and free men and women the cosmic reality could not be split up into a spiritual and a material dimension, it is clear that their famous spirituals have neither an exclusively spiritual and religious nor an exclusively political and material dimension. It is not a matter of either-or but of both-and. The singing of 'Steal away to Jesus' was originally the announcement of a secret night meeting, but the significance of this song does not end there. 'O Canaan, sweet Canaan, I am bound for the land of Canaan' was originally a song about the free North, but at the same time this song contains more than a coded political protest. The dualism in the white Christian concept of freedom came up against incomprehension and opposition among these people of African descent. The longing for freedom as expressed in the spirituals has several layers and dimensions, which usually escaped the white masters. This is expressed very evocatively in the song:

We'll soon be free,
    When de Lord will call us home.
My brudder, how long,
    'Fore we done sufferin' here?
It won't be long
    'Fore de Lord will call us home.
We'll walk de miry road
    Where pleasure never dies.
We'll walk de golden street
    Where pleasure never dies.
My brudder, how long,   ·
    'Fore we done sufferin' here?

We'll soon be free
　　When Jesus sets us free.
We'll fight for liberty
　　When de Lord will call us home.

(b) Black theology in the United States

Black theology is a product of the black revolution of the 1960s. Martin Luther King Jr and Malcolm X were the charismatic leaders in this decisive period of Afro-American history. Rarely has the word 'charismatic' been so appropriate: both embody, each in his own way, the radical élan of this time, not only as political but also as religious leaders of their people.

Spurred on by the vision of the 'beloved community', King showed the indissoluble connection between Christian *agape* (love) and social justice: deeply convinced that the goal could only be realized by means which accorded with it, in his strategy of non-violent resistance derived from the Sermon on the Mount and Gandhi he anticipated a future without domination and violence; he prophetically proclaimed that the time for radical change had come, but like the biblical prophets he had to discover that his mission was a failure.

Malcolm X had in common with King the fact that he too was the son of a Baptist preacher; however, in contrast to Martin with his relatively protected youth, Malcolm had personal experience of the harsh struggle for survival of the black city proletariat. In prison he was converted to the strict nationalism of the Black Muslims; in contrast to King's policy of integration into white society, Malcolm X asserted the right of blacks to self-determination, including the right of defence against the white aggressor with all necessary means. Moreover, neither the insights of Martin Luther King nor those of Malcolm X were new in the history of black people: without doubt the militant patience of King and his followers represents the mainstream in the history of black opposition, but from the violent slave rebellions to the appearance of Marcus Garvey at the beginning of this century, the aggressive nationalism of Malcolm X has been constantly present as an undercurrent.

In 1966 this nationalism gained the upper hand for the first time. The high expectations which King had aroused with his dream – a dream rooted in the ideals of the American bourgeois revolution – were not fulfilled. The cause of this failure did not lie with King and his followers, for the massive non-violent demonstrations were impressive enough. The courage and patience of the countless demonstrators, however, mercilessly revealed the intense violence of white racism, and after more than ten years of struggle for equal civil rights it became increasingly clear to Martin Luther King (one need only think of his position in the Vietnam war) that racism was no chance accident of American democracy but was closely connected with its economic, political and ideological structures. By then, though, much younger leaders had already departed from King's strategy and opted for Black Power.

This call for Black Power, which was issued for the first time in 1966 – a year after the murder of Malcolm X! – was a virulent reaction to the incapsulation of the civil rights movement by the white establishment. The slogan conveyed emotional overtones rather than a well-thought out and coherent strategy. However, the profuse revolutionary rhetoric, which above all served as a purge to feelings, should not make us forget that there were in fact fundamental political and strategical options involved which were deeply rooted both in the particularity of black history and in the universality of the ultimate questions of human life. As well as being a political movement, Black Power was a religious movement, and the charisma of its spiritual father Malcolm X clearly expressed the fact that all the central ideas of this black revolution were already fully present in what he wrote and said: self-determination, dependence, cultural revolution, national unity and self-government. What the Sermon on the Mount and Gandhi meant for the civil rights movement, the autobiography of Malcolm X and Franz Fanon's *The Wretched of the Earth* meant for the leaders of Black Power.

The rise of this movement proved a heavy burden for the black church – we use this last term here as a sociological collective term for the different black church denominations and for black Christians in predominantly white churches. Black church leaders had been to the fore in the demonstrations for equal civil rights. However, the young militant leaders had not failed to note the bitter scorn which Malcolm X poured on Christianity. Their departure from non-violent resistance was also a departure from the black church, which hitherto had occupied a unique place in the history of the people. The black church had been the only place where black people had their own worth and identity, where those who were trapped and humiliated during the week could experience on Sunday the liberating effect of the Spirit in the proclamation of the word of encouragement and consolation, and where their anger and frustration could be released in prayer, in the rhythm of song and dance, and in the ecstasy of the experience of conversion. For the Black Panthers and student leaders, by contrast, the black church had become the symbol of white domination, an instrument in the hands of the white authorities aimed at reconciling black men and women to their inhuman fate in the name of Christian love and reconciliation.

Indisputably there was occasion for harsh criticism. The black churches were not up to the immensely complex problems of modern industrialized society; many preachers took refuge in a timeless, moralistic preaching, or figured more as local status symbols than as spiritual leaders in the daily struggle for survival. These circumstances, which led many ghetto dwellers to seek their salvation in sects like that of Father Divine, compromised the black church as a whole, and even militant leaders felt confused.

The publication of *Black Religion: The Negro and Christianity in the United States*, a study by the black sociologist of religion Joseph R. Washington, which appeared in 1964, contributed quite substantially to this confusion. In two respects the author's argument was extremely provocative to black church leaders: 1. Washington's view was that the commitment to freedom and social justice characteristic of the black church at the time of slavery had given place to a strong materialism, coupled with disputes over church politics and organizational preoccupations; 2. the main point made by the book was that there was no theological reflection in the black church and that as a result it in fact stood outside the Christian tradition, since in the author's view an authentic Christian community needs to occupy a recognizable place in the Western theological tradition. Washington came to different conclusions in other more recent publications, but in *Black Religion* his view was that integration into American Protestantism is the only solution for the black church, and that it is the task of the white church and theology to make this possible.

The publication of *Black Religion* was important for the rise of present-day black theology in two ways. 1. Because Washington – going against current views – in any case assigns a place and function of its own to the historical phenomenon of black religion, he called for basic reflection on the relationship between black religion, Christian faith and social justice; 2. by his view that the black church has no theology he provoked black church leaders and theologians to demonstrate the opposite: 'If we were going to protect the Black commuity from Washington's promotion of this widely held White thesis that the Black church had no theology, then we needed to give some intellectual structure to the implicit Black Theology that we claimed was already present in the history of the Black Church' (James H.Cone).

But despite everything, the black churches continued to be part of ghetto life, and quite often the preachers were directly involved in the revolts in the long hot summers; they felt bound to the black city proletariat, and although they had all been active in King's non-violent movement, they did not want to yield to the strong pressure from the white side to agree with King in his condemnation of Black Power as a nihilistic movement. These church leaders and preachers were in fact the vehicles of what was to manifest itself in 1969 as black theology. In terms of organization this group emerged for the first time on 31 July 1966, when it issued a declaration of solidarity with Black Power, which was published in the *New York Times*. The group called itself the National Committee of Negro Churchmen, a name which was later changed to National Conference of Black Churchmen (NCBC).

However, the solidarity with Black Power did not mean that the link with Martin Luther King was broken. Rather, anyone who reads the declarations of NCBC from this time will get the impression that the group tried to build a bridge between the nationalism of the new movement and the integralism of the civil rights movement. However on no account would people abandon King. In the last resort he was the man who had given back to the black church its strength to fight; he was the one who in the tradition of the prophets had proclaimed the *kairos*, the time of fulfilment: *now* the day had dawned for America to fulfil its promises of democracy; *now* was the time to climb out of the dark, abandoned valley of segregation to the sunlit path of racial justice.

With his dream, King was able to conjure up an intense and positive tension between history, the *de facto* situation of violence and racist delusion, and eschatology, the expectation of the beloved community. And if it is true that any form of theology (liberation theology) stands or falls by daring to resolve the tension between history and eschatology, particularity and universality, then black theology owes its stimulus towards liberation in the first place to King.

It must be pointed out here that for the last two years of his life this great man feverishly looked for new ways; he also increasingly realized the economic roots of racism and the reality of American imperialism (Vietnam); he became more radical, and felt himself more closely associated with the struggle for liberation among colonized people in Africa and elsewhere. But not only he but also Malcolm X was involved in a radical reorientation shortly before his death. Just as Martin increasingly saw the shortcomings of his policy of integration, so Malcolm, after his journey to Mecca in 1964, distanced himself from the narrow nationalism of the Black Muslims. Without doubt both, each in his own way, were involved in a process of radicalization which would have brought them closer together had they not been murdered.

So far, Afro-American history has twice experienced a *kairos*, a moment when liberation seems to be a tangible reality. However, both times the *kairos* remained unfulfilled. The abolition of slavery after the end of the American civil war, which had aroused the expectation of black people enormously, was followed by a period of rigid segregation which in some respects was even worse than slavery. The second *kairos* of the black revolution in the 1960s was followed by a severe relapse in the 1970s. The gains in both the civil rights struggle and Black Power seemed almost exclusively to have benefited an élite; the situation of the black city proletariat was more hopeless than ever. Black people are now waiting for a third *kairos*. But this waiting can never be passive: liberation does not come by itself, but has to be fought for. Among young militant politicians, historians and theologians there is a growing conviction that the rapprochement between Martin and Malcolm before their deaths contained a promise and obligation for the future. Integration has proved as hopeless a way as nationalism or separatism. Both tendencies, which keep cropping up in Afro-American history – nationalism sometimes in reaction to a failure to integrate or to a time of severe repression – must go together.

The precondition for a synthesis of this kind, however, is a real analysis of society which cannot be found in a developed form either in Martin or in Malcolm, an analysis which does justice to the complex problem of the relationship of racism to the struggle over class and sex. Strategically, what is needed above all is to build a position of unity and power – this is where the nationalistic element comes in – in order to enter into coalitions – the integrating element – with other ethnic minorities, with radical political groupings, with the women's movement, the peace movement or the ecological movement.

In this context of the struggle for a third *kairos*, black theology, on its own ground, can make a modest but essential contribution, through its critical function within the black church and society, towards ensuring the rise and continuation of a prophetic tension between history and eschatology, particularity and universality. If the tension snaps in favour of one pole, eschatology, then all that is left is a belief in the hereafter which flees from the world; if the tension snaps in favour of the other pole, history, then a pessimistic realism gains the upper hand which no longer believes in a new heaven and a new earth; the pseudo-*universalism* of a general and therefore abstract ethic of love and reconciliation predominates, beyond question at the expense of specific experiences of oppression, suffering and conflict. If that then stands over against the *particularity* of a black struggle which is not related to the universal dimension of the salvation of all men and women, there may be talk of a struggle for survival which calls for wholehearted respect, but it will not be a struggle for true liberation – though, 'We cannot be free until they are free' (James Baldwin).

This prophetic, liberating tension is no stranger to the black experience of faith. It is tangibly present in the old slave songs which are often rightly compared with the biblical psalms. Similarly, it can be recognized in the words and actions of men and women like Harriet Tubman, Sojourner Truth, David Walker and Henry McNeal Turner. Black theology is therefore perhaps primarily a new articulation of an experience of faith which is as old as black history itself, the experience that,

I'm a chile of God wid my soul set free,
For Christ hab bought my liberty.

Black theology owes its origin to Black Power. The struggle for Black Power arose out of the concern of black people to take matters into their own hands, to be the subjects of their own history. 'Powerlessness produces a people of beggars', wrote the black church leaders in their first declaration. It is a consequence of the specific dynamics of the race struggle that Black Consciousness can be used as a synonym for Black Power: power is in the first place self-awareness, 'the courage to be' in a hostile environment in which blackness is synonymous with inferiority.

This struggle for self assertion, for power, called for theological reflection, all the more where the dominant theology and social ethics rejected Black Power in the name of the gospel. However, the theological reflection was part of the problem; the theoretical field covered by academic theology was occupied by *white* power; there was no room for the experiences and questions of those people for whom the black church had a direct responsibility: the unemployed, drug addicts, prisoners, people who led a marginalized and hopeless existence in the Great Society of Lyndon B.Johnson and who rebelled against it because they knew deep in their hearts that this situation was sinful and in conflict with God's will. The dominant theology was white; in other words, it was quite oblivious to the experience of the black person in his or her history with God; in their studies, the few black theological students present heard only of Bultmann, Barth and Niebuhr, and nothing of their own culture and history – simply because this was thought to be theologically irrelevant.

Among the church leaders who had come together in NCBC there was unanimity over their own need for theological reflection on questions of power, violence, liberation and reconciliation. However, it took until 1969 to get that far. Then *Black Theology and Black Power* appeared, from the young and hitherto unknown theologian James H.Cone. This book, which had more the character of an angry pamphlet, achieved precisely what the black church leaders had hoped for: with its fierce polemic it made a breach in the closed ranks of the white theological discussions and created room for a distinctive critical reflection on the black experience, the black struggle and black history.

Cone's theology, in *Black Theology and Black Power* concentrated in provocative sentences which gave this book its force, can be best characterized in dogmatic terms as a pneumatological christology: all the emphasis is put on the living, active presence of the God who became man, indeed slave; the God who takes the side of the poor and the maltreated. In America, seared by the racial struggle in the long hot summers, Christ is present in the burning ghettoes to identify himself with black people, who seek to liberate themselves from the inferior image that white society has imposed on them. Black Power is essentially concerned with the liberation of black humanity, and this struggle is not only in accord with the gospel of Jesus Christ, but is actually the expression of the gospel.

The provocative polemical tone of *Black Theology and Black Power* has led some theologians to see black theology as little more than an emotional outburst, perhaps understandable and justified in itself, but dominated too much by the mood of Black Power to be worth taking seriously as theology. But quite apart from misunderstanding the function of the book – namely to open up hitherto enclosed theoretical terrain and make room for black experience and reflection – these critics have also failed to note that James H.Cone is a typically dialectical thinker who, however articulate and 'one-sided' his writing may be, knows that any theological reflection is fragmentary and moves between thesis and antithesis, never being capable of grasping the synthesis, the liberating praxis of Christ himself. The fact that white theologians – with a few exceptions – have so notably missed the depth of Cone's theology arises from the very subject matter of his book: that the dominant theology is 'white' because, for the most part unconsciously, it reproduces the prevailing power relationships, in which there is no place for black experience and reflection.

Black theology has already come a long way from *Black Theology and Black Power* in 1969 to the present day. Cone's book led to important discussions among black theologians, for example those between him and J.Deotis Roberts on the relationship between liberation and reconciliation. However, the chief criticism of Cone was that he was still too much under the influence of what he was opposed to, namely academic theology. Gayraud S.Wilmore, Cecil Cone and the black historian of religion Charles Long criticized Cone because the insights of Barth, Bonhoeffer, Moltmann, Sartre and Camus were further to the fore in his book than the historical experience of blacks. The same criticism was also directed against Cone's second book, *A Black Theology of Liberation*, which appeared soon after the first and is more systematic in aim. In this book Paul Tillich's method of correlation dominates to such an extent that neither the historical character of the biblical narratives nor the uniqueness of black experience is sufficiently given its due. The third book, *The Spirituals and the Blues: An Interpretation*, was written to counter criticism which Cone himself felt to be justified. However, Cone's markedly christo-logical interpretation of slave songs and stories did not convince many of his colleagues. The question arises whether as a systematic theologian he does not impose the norm of his theologizing, Jesus Christ the living Lord, too strongly on his historical source material and thus fails to do justice to the specifically African elements in religious experience and the experience of black slaves and their descendants. Gayraud S.Wilmore made much of the active presence of African influences in his masterly study *Black Religion and Black Radicalism*, which appeared in 1972 and showed more strongly than Cone's roughly contemporaneous study the ambivalence of black religion, which was a source not only of rebellion and radical opposition, but also of disquiet and alienation.

In 1975, with the appearance of Cone's fourth and in our view most important book so far, *God of the Oppressed*, a second phase in black theology began. It was now possible to see the effect of the intensive contacts which black theologians had meanwhile made with theologians from Africa, Asia and Latin America. The methodological and hermeneutical questions which are decisive for liberation theology as a new way of doing theology are fully dealt with in this book. Cone's main position here is that 'one's social and historical context decides not only the questions we address to God but also the mode or form of the answers given to the question'; from here questions arise about the relationship of theory and praxis, contextuality and theological existence, as a positive choice in what is always an ideological struggle. His most recent book, *My Soul Looks Back* (1982), a biographical retrospect on the course he has followed so far, shows how fruitful have been the encounters with American feminist theologians and with liberation theologians who have banded together in EATWOT. The wider perspective that this has given black theology, sharpening its insights into the historical reality of capitalism and imperialism, has not, however, been at the expense of its original commitment within the black church and community. This community remains the framework within which black theology stands or falls.

Black theology is an attempt to understand the situation of black people, the victims of centuries of racism, in the light and under the judgment of God's word in Jesus Christ. The more they are able to gain theoretical ground in what has been shown to be 'white' theology, the less has been their need for polemic, and features that were already present and presupposed from the beginning come to the fore: it is evident that the no of polemical repudiation is simply the underside of the establisment's yes. Although black theology takes very seriously the history of the suffering of the black slaves and their descendants, in the last instance it is a joyful, glad discipline, because it knows that in the history of the Jew Jesus of Nazareth the white death is overcome. This positive yes finds its most evocative expression in the saying 'Christ is black'.

This confession need not arouse feelings of alienation or anxiety. Some theologians, who have never had personal experience of the reality of racism, have branded it as 'racism in reverse'. Nothing is further from the truth.

Let us look more closely at the significance of the predicate 'black' when applied to Christ. The first thing we must realize here is that talk of the black Messiah takes place in the social and historical context of white racism. The confession does not express an eternal abstract truth, but applies to situations in which so-called racial characteristics determine people's social positions. In a society where a black skin is the dominant factor, these people are daily confronted with exploitation and humiliation, and the 'emptying' of the Messiah Jesus which is celebrated in the psalm in Philippians 2.6-11 means that Christ becomes black, i.e. he takes the form of people who are treated as non-persons.

The expression 'Christ is black', specific though it may be, is not exclusive. It does not exclude the need to say other things in other situations. Thus it is an example of contextual theology which, on the basis of the incarnation of the Word, dares to confess that in a situation where the colour of a person's skin determines his or her opportunities in life, the gospel is not colour blind.

In *God of the Oppressed* James H.Cone makes one more thing clear, that the blackness of Christ is confessed on the basis of Luke 4.18f., where Jesus is the anointed who proclaims the good news to the poor, and Matt.25.45, 'Truly, I say to you, in so much as you have not done this to one of the least of these my children, you have not done it to me.' Thus his blackness is not a projection: 'Christ is black, therefore, not because of some cultural or psychological need of black people, but because and only because Christ *really* enters into our world where the poor, the despised and the black are, disclosing that he is with them, enduring their humiliation and pain, and transforming oppressed slaves into liberating servants.' Cone also replies to those theologians who think that Christ's blackness seriously endangers the universal significance of the gospel: 'Indeed their insistence upon the universal note of the gospel arises out of their own particular political and social interests. As long as they can be sure that the gospel is for everybody, ignoring that God liberated a particular people from Egypt, came into a particular man called Jesus, and for the particular purpose of liberating the oppressed, then they can continue to talk in theological abstractions, failing to recognize that such talk is not the gospel unless it is related to the concrete freedom of the little ones.'

It is not unimportant to note that the notion of Christ's blackness is not an invention of James H.Cone or Gayraud S.Wilmore: it is deeply rooted in black faith and history. However much many black Christians, too, over the course of history, have internalized the picture of the white Christ, we need also to note another tendency. Already at the time of the invisible church in the period of slavery, black slaves refused to accept that the figure of Christ as it came to them from the biblical stories could have the white features of the slave owners. It is notable that however strict and patriarchal may have been the God whom the white missionaries proclaimed on the plantations, for the slaves Jesus was a figure of trust, an intimate friend who knew their pain and worries. They recognized themselves in his suffering, and the torture which he had to endure was all too familiar to them:

> Were you there when they crucified my Lord?
>> were you there when they crucified my Lord?
> Oh! sometimes it causes me to tremble, tremble, tremble;
>> were you there when they crucified my Lord?

Even after the period of slavery this identification with the sufferings of Christ remained. In 1929, the year of the Great Depression, the black poet Countee Cullen wrote a long narrative poem of 963 lines entitled 'The Black Christ'; it begins like this:

> How Calvary in Palestine
> Extending down to me and mine
> Was but the first leaf in a line
> of trees on which a Man should swing
> World without end, in suffering
> For all men's healing, let me sing.

Perhaps because Good Friday is such a tangible reality in the black community, the joy of Easter is only really expressed at Pentecost; black worship is concerned above all with the presence of the Spirit, who takes total (even physical) possession of the weary and heavy-laden and gives them new strength, in the conviction that the promised land is near in which people will no longer be judged by the colour of their skin but by their character, and in which the words of the old slave song which King quoted at the end of his dream in 1963 have become reality: 'Free at last! Free at last! Great God Almighty, we are free at last!'

(*c*) Black theology in the South African system of apartheid

> How good and joyful it is to be healed from the devastating
> sickness of racism and division;
> and to live together without dissonance as God's people.

The spirit of the Lord will fill the hearts and understanding of all people.

No one shall be judged any longer by their race or the colour of their skin.

But all will be governed in justice and faithfulness.

War will end, and everyone will rebuild the land together.

People will take no account of the colour of skin.

For all will be regarded as people of God, whom he made in his image.

And that will be the beginning of what the Lord has promised – eternal life!

This reading – 'version' is far too superficial, uncommitted a word – of Psalm 133 by Zephaniah Kameeta, a preacher in Namibia, is a model of contextual theology. The universal eschatological vision developed here is born out of the quite specific context of apartheid. Racism, war and violence make up the *de facto* situation in which this psalm is used, and only *in* this situation does the psalm take on the enormous tension between eschatology and history, particularity and universality, which, as we have seen earlier, is the hallmark of any authentic liberation theology.

At any rate, the confession of this universal vision of the future within the context of the South African system of apartheid is a specific act of opposition; it implies a partisan choice against the whites in power and for all those who lead a marginalized existence because their skins are black.

This universality of reconciliation between the races does not conceal the existing situation of injustice and exploitation, but shows up its inhumanity and godlessness; this eschatology is not a flight from reality but the expression of a specific polemical standpoint.

What happens in this reading of Psalm 133 is symptomatic of the hermeneutics of black liberation theology in the South African system of apartheid. It can be said that Kameeta understands the biblical psalm in the light of the situation, just as conversely he understands his situation in the light of the psalm. However, that is to put it too superficially, for in fact something much more decisive is happening: *the situation brings the psalm to life.* Kameeta is not functioning here as the classical theologian who mediates between the Bible and the newspaper and whose individual subjectivity mediates between what was said in scripture *then* and what must be said in the present situation *now*. He is more a receiver than a mediator: *in* the situation this biblical text speaks to him; it is not he but the situation itself that interprets the text as a meaningful totality. The situation is the historical context which brings the text to life.

However, the situation, too, must be expressed and indicated in more detail. For 'situation' or 'historical context' here are not amorphous concepts, but focus on a reality which is experienced and analysed as oppressive, killing, perverted. In a particular situation the psalm speaks to a particular situation, or rather, it speaks against it. As such, as opposition, the text embodies the hope and expectation of black women, men and children who through the countless discriminatory laws and practices of the system of apartheid are reminded of their inferiority and political immaturity from cradle to grave. The questions and answers of black people about the possibility or impossibility of Christian belief and action are determined not by the historical context in general but by this specific context of suffering, oppression and dependence in a world of apartheid. Thus for South African black theology, which seeks to be rooted in the black experience and struggle, the 'ordinary' daily reality (which in fact is extremely extraordinary) of black people is the hermeneutical *locus* – a reality which on the one hand is dominated by an inhuman system imposed by a white minority on a majority with the support of international capital, and on the other hand is characterized by the struggle for another society in which no one will ever again be judged by their race or the colour of their skin.

This hermeneutical position puts black theology on a par with other forms of liberation theology, and in its own specific way this black theology shows that hermeneutical and methodological starting points are decisive for the way in which theological work functions in the context of church and society. This is what the black theologian and Lutheran bishop Manas Buthelezi meant when in a series of lectures which he gave in Heidelberg in the summer of 1972 he characterized 'black theology' as 'merely a methodological concept of a technique for doing theology'. Somewhat misleadingly in this connection he spoke of a theology with an 'anthropological approach', by which he meant that black theology takes as its starting point specific everyday reality, history as people daily experience it together:

> Blackness is an anthropological fact which utterly governs my whole existence day by day: it determines where I live, whom I meet and with whom I can share my daily life. Everyday life unfolds before me within the limits and range of possibilities inherent in the black situation. The word of God speaks to me where I in fact am, in my blackness. I can only go to a black church, and usually the service can only be taken by someone who is black, as I am.

When Manas Buthelezi speaks of an anthropological approach, he does not mean anthropology as an academic discipline. He opposes forms of 'indigenous' or 'African' theology as practised by white scholars like Placide Tempels and Bengt Sundkler; he calls their approach to African reality 'ethnographic', objecting that it essentially makes 'African man', 'African culture', 'the African spirit' an object, a static construct from a romanticized past, at the expense of the dynamic, concrete reality of the present. Buthelezi's 'anthropological approach' is opposed to this, and takes its starting point in the specific historical reality as black people experience it every day in the system of apartheid; blackness becomes a theological problem because it is a factor, indeed the determining factor, in their daily existence. To speak of God's revelation in Jesus Christ outside this determining factor means *de facto* that revelation stands outside history as experienced by people in a given place and in a given situation – and in this way the incarnation, God's being made man, becomes an abstract object of theological speculation instead of a living reality – living by virtue of the resurrection and the outpouring of the Spirit – which determines our history.

The fact that black theology is serious about daily life, specific history as people make it and experience it, as the *locus* of theology, the place where God speaks and acts, does not mean that here for the umpteenth time in the history of Christian theology what Karl Barth fought against all his life actually happens, i.e. revelation becomes a predicate of history and – apart from the Word of God in Jesus Christ which is revealed to us in scripture – 'nature' and 'history' are places where God can be found by human knowledge. For black theology, revelation is not a predicate of history simply because empirical reality clearly raised the question asked by William R. Jones in the title of his book which appeared in 1973: *Is God a White Racist?*. History as black people have to experience it does not *intrinsically* point either to a good creation or to a God of love and mercy. In this connection, in his introduction to the Dutch edition of the symposium *Black Theology in South Africa*, Dr J.J.Buskes rightly points out that it is remarkable 'that the blacks in South Africa who have had to put up with so much evil have taken over the gospel from those who did this evil to them, and despite the fact that there was no end to the evil, did not cease to be Christians but remained Christians, perhaps precisely as a result of their anger at white Christianity and the God of that white Christianity, the God of colonialism, the God of Vorster (subjective genitive), who whatever else is certainly not the God and Father of Jesus Christ (objective and subjective genitive), and that the blacks who accuse this church as being a markedly colonial and racist institution (a black Christian may not marry a white Christian woman nor may he take part in the eucharist in the church of the whites), despite this church but thanks to the gospel have remained Christians.'

Black theology is only saved from being a 'blood and soil' theology by being a theology of the oppresed who have no interests of their own (quite the contrary) in a heroic nationalist and idealistic interpretation of history because this (*a*) is precisely what they are opposed to and (*b*) inevitably relies on 'ordinances of creation' given by God which in practice always support the ruling powers and cripple the gospel as good news for the poor.

Moreover, the hermeneutical problem of the relationship between 'text' and 'context' was not raised by a black theologian like Allan Boesak in order to provide a theological justification for allowing the historical context to dominate over the text, but precisely in order to show up the way in which white theology in its hermeneutical innocence has in fact always allowed the white context to dominate the text by diverting or rejecting the partisan support of the gospel story for the wretched of the earth. Of course the historical situation is the linchpin of black theology, but it is understood in the light of the Word of God incarnate in Jesus of Nazareth: black situation and experience are therefore not absolutized, but are illuminated critically and prophetically

– and this means 'that the praxis of liberation is ultimately judged not by the demands of the situation but by the liberating gospel of Jesus Christ' (Boesak).

On the other hand, Barth's insight that revelation is not a predicate of history but on the contrary that history is a predicate of revelation – in other words, that we only learn what history is from the Word revealed in scripture – is not free from the danger that the specific present-day reality becomes a kind of vacuum 'between the times', between Christ's coming and his return. This danger is not present so much in Barth himself, since he did not hesitate to adopt political positions and the great volumes of the *Church Dogmatics* go far more deeply into the events of the time and are far more contextual than people often suppose. However, it is present among those theologians who think that they have learned from Barth that in all circumstances theology must note the 'eschatological proviso' by guarding against any form of identification of gospel and historical reality, of the kingdom of God and social and political movements, parties and positions.

However, this eschatological proviso, though intrinsically correct, induces a profound fear of entering the deep troubled waters of contemporary historical and social relationships and conflicts. People prefer to stand safely on the dry land of a biblical theology which can give a splendid account of the way in which God's *debarim* (words and acts) initiate and constitute 'history' in an authentic sense in the time of Moses, Micah and Paul but maintain a diffident silence on the prophetic question where these *debarim*, this salvation history, is present and can be found nowadays. History (salvation history) is thus reduced to being a phenomenon from the time of the Bible, in other words, to past time: in that case theology is little more than archaeology, and pneumatology remains the most neglected chapter of Christian dogmatics. Moreover – although in theory people argue to the contrary – inevitably this theology remains indebted to an unbiblical dualism because in practice safe doctrine gets the better of the risky ambiguities of life, and the theory of the church's confession comes before the praxis of Christian action. Despite Barth, dogmatics and ethics are kept quite separate.

Like any contemporary theology of liberation, black theology in South Africa is steeped in the need to overcome this dualism. It has discovered the extent to which this dualism and the individualism which goes with it have been instrumental in alienating African Christians, not simply from their own culture and situation, but also from the content and structure of the biblical narratives. And it is all too aware of the extent to which the dependence of this theological way of thinking imposed from outside is making the black church increasingly irrelevant to the growing school-children, women and men in Soweto and Crossroads.

So its first action is to refuse to exploit the reality of God's Word in Jesus Christ dualistically against the black reality in South Africa. It seeks to break right through the imported word-games of theological concepts and categories in order to be able to find a way through to the reality of life as it is actually lived, to the daily reality of an oppressed people. And the central question is how the messianic reality of the Risen One is present in the life of this people.

All intrinsically relevant theological discussions about the concept of history and the relationship between salvation and history cannot prevent black theology from raising this central question with great pertinacity. Black theology cannot deny itself the theological right to look for and struggle for the unity and wholeness of life, in line with African feelings – against the dominant discursive and academic thought in which reality is analysed, categorized, defined and regulated. For black theology, the biblical account and the African experience coincide in that liberation is related to the totality of human existence, or rather, to the fullness of life in community.

This concern for inclusiveness and totality can already be found in the first beginnings of black theology in the South African context. It is worth noting that this theology was not introduced to South Africa by professional theologians or church leaders, but by students of the University Christian Movement, a mixed organization which was banned in 1972, and by the South African Student Organization set up in 1969, of which the unforgettable Steve Biko was the first president. The collection *Black Theology in South Africa*, mentioned earlier, arose out of this student movement, but was banned by the South African government directly after its appearance. Although it is indisputably true that the South African authors recognized themselves in the work of James H.Cone and other Afro-American theologians, their theological work has clear contours of its own, which are of course connected with the difference between the North American and South African context. From the beginning, black theology in South Africa was closely connected with the black consciousness movement, which was similarly supported by black students. 'As the philosophy and praxis of black liberation, black consciousness is indissolubly connected with black theology' (Takatso A.Mofokeng).

The connection between black theology, black consciousness and the concern for totality mentioned above has been discussed systematically by Mokgethi Motlhabi:

> Black theology is that aspect of black consciousness which seeks to relate God and the whole of the religious values to the black man in his situation precisely as a 'black man' in South Africa. To be black in our country means in the first place to be the victim of 'apartheid' – to be the object of colonization, disinheritance and exploitation. It also means, in religious circles, to be pagan, barbaric and almost damned; and all these because of the colour of one's skin, which is not white. In black theology the term only secondarily connotes colour, which popular white parlance prefers to call 'non-white'. It denotes all the oppressed people in our country irrespective of colour (which cannot be white, of course), nationality or creed. It thus embraces all the African people, the Indians and the so-called Coloureds. Black theology, therefore, seeks to relate God as both man's creator and liberator to all these people in their entire situation, not only the religious, but also the social, the political and the economic situations. God's word and sustenance permeates through the whole of man's life and being by virute of his very creation (in the image of God)... In black theology man is regarded as a complete whole, a mind-body-soul composite in, and confronted by, a complete situation.

Its intention, in the light of the liberating messianic story, of demythologizing the reductionist arguments of the dominant white power and advancing towards *complete* reality with all the flagrant violation of human values and justice comprised in it, in fact makes that black theology no more and no less a commitment than the identity and structure of Christian belief itself. It raises basic questions which are of decisive importance for the world church as a whole, and in this way it is *par excellence ecumenical* theology.

It is all the more to be regretted that there was no possibility of developing further and deepening, through considered publications, this first approach, which was embodied in articles and readings on different questions. The only extended studies of black theology so far are the Kampen dissertations by Allan Boesak and T.Mofokeng. The South African government soon recognized the danger of this way of doing theology and intervened in its usual fashion: black theology was killed off by being banned (the prohibition of publications, house arrest and so on). The privilege of being able to speak and write about black theology unhindered within South Africa is reserved for whites.

In Chapter 8 of the notorious Schlebusch/Le Grange Report which appeared in May 1975 and led to the abolition and condemnation of the Christian Institute, black theology was described as the theological arm of Black Power and as a means of propaganda for a revolutionary Marxist ideology. This report has been published, and anyone who so wishes can note its content. However, the refutation of it by Manas Buthelezi, *Black Theology and the Le Grange-Schlebusch Commission, Pro Veritate*, Vol.13, no.6, October 1975, 4-6, is forbidden reading in South Africa.

That theological paladins of apartheid like C.W.A.Boshoff attack black theology fiercely is not surprising. The only surprising thing is the low level on which the attacks are made. It is even sadder that the publications of white South African theologians who in principle have a positive view of black theology are not in a position really to do justice to its intentions. One example is the pamphlet by D.J.Bosch, professor of missiology, which appeared in Holland in 1974; the last chapter deals with trends in South African black theology (this chapter appeared earlier in an abbreviated and heavily censored form in *Pro Veritate*). In contrast to Schlebusch/Le Grange, Bosch stresses the difference between South African black theology and the American black theology of James H.Cone; moreover, within the South African version he distinguishes at least four different directions. Whatever interest may be served by these distinctions, academic clarity is certainly not. What is the point of identifying different trends in a movement which clearly presents itself as a unity and which, certainly in 1974, was no more than a first beginning after which anything was still possible, thus assigning individual theologians to particular positions and making them differ from one another? Does not this method, which fixes in a static way what is very much a dynamic movement, conflict with the subject-matter it seeks to understand and clarify? Of course there are differences, and these need to be recognized and not trivialized. But the vital thing is to see that black theology, like any theology of liber-ation, implies a methodological and hermeneutical criticism of an absolutizing of conceptual thought in theology, in which the other (Other) is objectified and definitions, distinctions, categories have to give the illusion that people are dealing with living reality. Liberation theology does not argue for the abolition of conceptual, rational thought, but it does call for a recognition of its limitations. At the end of his argument Bosch says: 'One thing is clear; no less is expected of us than a new metanoia, a new radical conversion.' If such a sentence is meant seriously and is not an all too facile edifying slogan, then Dr D.J.Bosch must relate this conversion first of all to the methodological and hermeneutical presuppositions of his own theologizing.

Vital though black theology in South Africa may be, the mostly underground character of its activities does not help us to follow its development. We have the impression that the concern of black theologians is at present directed towards three groups of problems which in part overlap.

First of all, black theologians put great emphasis on biblical proclamation – more strongly than, for example, in Latin Amer-ican theology. When black theologians and preachers like Desmond Tutu and Allan Boesak argue that reconciliation and liberation, love and justice belong together, they do so on the basis of biblical theology. 'If reconciliation is the transformation of people and the world in which we live, then reconciliation indeed signifies liberation. Belief in Jesus Christ is concerned with God in his liberating and reconciling acts. Only when someone is really free does he begin to understand the need for reconciliation and can he become God's instrument.' It is much too simplistic to say that this remark by Allan Boesak is the result of a selective reading of the Bible in which the exodus theme, the social protest of the prophets and Luke 4.18f. are predominant at the expense of other biblical ideas and motives. Boesak is concerned here with the heart of the gospel, with that by which everything stands or falls. And it is precisely this nucleus which is misunderstood and vitiated in the theory and practice of apartheid, at the very point where apartheid tries to give itself Christian and theological legitimation.

The problem of biblical interpretation is not a matter of being one-sided or less one-sided; it involves the hermeneutical question of the eyes we use to read scripture. Are they those of the powerful who have everything to lose, viz. their riches, or are they those of the small and insignificant? Black theology has no pretensions to be the theology of an intellectual black élite. Now more than ten years ago, Bonganjalo Goba wrote in an essay on 'Corporate Personality in Ancient Israel and Africa': 'We blacks in the South African situation can no longer live as isolated individuals. Our highest loyalty must be to our black community, and that is what we seek in our need for black solidarity. This is the significance of the concept of corporate personality in the South Africa today.' This loyalty means that this corporate personality – the individual represents the community and achieves fulfilment only within this community - is the real subject of black theology. In turn that means that black professional theologians must take seriously as a source of theological knowledge the experiences and expressions of the faith of oppressed people as these take shape in spontaneous songs, prayers and in the popular theatre. The people has a christology of its own which is the opposite to belief in the white God of apartheid: Jesus is a 'soul brother' who knows what suffering, humiliation and oppresion mean because he experienced these things himself and still experiences them through his identification with 'the least of his brothers'. Black theology can only be a theology *for*, on behalf of, the people, if it is also a theology *of* the people. In the fruitful tension between this 'for' and this 'of' we have the self-critical character of its work of theological reflection.

A third complex of problems follows from this last point. We can sum it up under the heading of an analysis and theory of society. If it is to be a theology for and of oppressed people, black theology must also recognize the historical causes and structures of this oppression. It must see that racism and apartheid are rooted in economic exploitation and class conflict, and at the same time it must recognize that in any context, racism as ideology, once evoked, begins to lead a life of its own and in turn influences economic and political relationships. Black theology must put the 'internal colonialism' in South Africa in the broad historical context of Western economic, political and ideological expansion, but at the same time it must also note the particular historical circumstances which have given the South African system of apartheid its specific form. Finally, it must investigate how the centuries-old history of exploitation and racism has affected the black people's experience of faith – in such a way that the last word is not with the mechanisms of oppression and the inhuman practices of the system in power but with the vital, challenging expectation of a different future.

Shun Govender, the present secretary of the Broederkring, put this last point in the following way:

> Our history is given meaning in an interpretation which lays bare the structures and traditions of oppressions which are operative within it. But it is given fundamental meaning by the people who cherish the burning hope of emerging on to the stage of a history they have participated in fashioning and in which they shall be free subjects – fully and truly human at last, open to the power of the future. Open to the historical possibilities and challenges of another tomorrow.

4

African Theology and Liberation from Cultural and Religious Domination

Only intrepid missiologists have so far ventured into the almost impenetrable jungle of African theology. Otherwise, European theology, elsewhere by no means averse to novelties, does not expose itself to the tropical downpour of articles, scripts, congress addresses and monographs which has finally been unleashed on the African continent after a long drought. Why this strange silence from the European side? Are African theologians less worthy of note than Gutiérrez or Míguez Bonino, M.M.Thomas or Kosuke Koyama?

Without doubt the age-old prejudices still take their toll. If attitudes towards the Asian East are determined by a deep and mysterious awe of the mystical refinement of its high religions and cultures, and Latin America at all events was regarded as a Christianized continent, darkest Africa remained in the European imagination a great morass, by-passed by the dynamics of civilization, and where ebullient pagan primitivism had its heyday. The well-known story by Edwin Smith about his conversation with the writer Emil Ludwig is still typical: when Ludwig heard that missionaries were busy putting Africans in touch with God, he was amazed and replied with the words, 'How can the uncivilized African have any idea of God? How is this possible?... Deity is a philosophical conception which they will find it impossible to comprehend.'

However, more is involved than the effect of this semi-conscious, deeply-rooted ethnocentrism. Latin American liberation theology and black theology are focussed on the future: exodus and the kingdom of peace and justice form their dynamic centre and represent liberation from the oppressive bonds of a repressive and systematic religiosity. In this respect, for all the hermeneutical differences, one might say that they converge with normative tendencies in European theology (to which, of course, liberation theologians owe a great deal); here, in the footsteps of the philosopher Ernst Bloch, radical subversive hope is shown to be a central theological category. This same Ernst Bloch also produced the insight that only an atheist can be a good Christian, and vice versa, that only a Christian can be a good atheist. In the light of this Blochian version of Marx's criticism of religion it was possible to understand the biblical witness as a challenge to abolish all *re-ligio*, every tie to a sacral, cultic heteronomy which legitimates the earthly master-servant relationship and social heteronomy – an abolition which serves to make men and women human!

At least on first acquaintance, the attempt by African theology to revalue its own ancient religious traditions is diametrically opposed to this effort, in the wake of Ernst Bloch, but also following Barth and Miskotte as theologians of the Word, to read scripture as anti-pagan, anti-religious witness. The African theologian seeks to cut free from the theological thought-modes and practices of faith imposed by the Western mission, which do touch the African's heart. It has set itself the task, to use the words of E.Bolaji Idowu (Nigeria) in the collection *Biblical Revelation and African Beliefs*, 'to find an answer to the delicate question whether there is any correlation between the biblical conception of God and the African conception of God, between what God has done and is busy doing according to the biblical tradition and doctrine and what God has done and is busy doing according to the traditional African practices of faith.' This way of posing the problem comprises a plea for *re-ligio*, for a new relationship between the gospel and the myths and rites of African peoples hallowed by tradition.

In past years, this link or correlation between the biblical witness and the African 'incurably religious' experience of reality has been sought and found in various ways. We shall return to that directly. However, the great question is whether and how far, in the light of the radical biblical criticism of religion, to look for this connection is not to return to the fleshpots of Egypt, to the land of old and new Pharaohs. Can the story of the exodus and a new future be given its due if it is set in the framework of traditional African religion and culture? Is not here, for the umpteenth time in history, the story of God's *dabar* (word/act) cramped by the framework of a religion and world-view which robs it of its liberating, renewing force? Does not African theology here succumb to the same seduction which has constantly weakened Western Christianity? Moreover, in the repristination of traditional religious forms is there not a dangerous romanticizing tendency, a nostalgic longing for the cyclical experience of reality in a pre-industrial agrarian culture? And does not this gaze towards the past represent a suspicious underestimation of the deep crisis and transitional period in which the African world at present finds itself? In short, is it not wrong to see African theology as a form of liberation theology in line with Latin American or Asian experiments in which the Bible is explicitly read as *biblia pauperum*, as the book of the liberation of the poor?

Like any form of theology which adopts an adjective – 'black', 'feminist' or 'Latin American' – African theology raises a particular question in ecumenical discusssion. Anyone who wants to gain access to this theology will do best first of all to have a keen awareness of this basic problem. If this principle is not observed, then there is an enormous risk that justice will not be done to the intentions of African theologians.

Contextual theology can only be understood contextually. It is not a matter of attacking African religious forms of expression with the preformed frameworks of a criticism of religion inspired by Marx or Bloch, Barth or Bonhoeffer, since these last were developed in the context of European Christianity and are directly valid only there. The usefulness of these forms of religious criticism for the African situation is at best indirect; in other words the question of their validity needs to be seen against the background of a careful analysis of the African historical and social context and the problems which arise there. At the very point where criticism of religion demonstrates that religious conceptions and practices are always 'produced' by human beings, and that human beings are not abstractions but live in specific social relationships which have grown up over history, it is impossible to escape the insight that generalizations about religion and its function as an opiate are dangerous nonsense.

Only contextual analysis of an always complex reality in

which economic, political-legal and ideological relationships are entangled in a complicated way can answer the question how far religious conceptions, traditions and customs alienate people from their own reality. Those who regard the 'incurable religiosity' of Africans as intrinsically alienating and outdated, are arguing on different presuppositions from those who used to argue that Africans were wild and pagan: here Eurocentrism has its heyday and the spiritual achievements of the West are regarded as the criterion by which African religious and cultural traditions and customs are to be measured.

Anyone who steeps himself in what has appeared in the last fifteen years in the name of African Christian theology or, in short, African theology, will have little difficulty in discovering what the basic problem is. It can be summed up in the word acculturation, the process of change which takes place when groups or peoples of different cultures come into direct contact with one another over a long period. From the beginning, the impact of the colonial powers and the pressure of their missionary activities on traditional African cultural patterns has had a strongly racist impact; the inferiority of the African 'natural man' to the civilized European was an established fact which was taken for granted; the African was regarded as a creature without culture and history. However different the political thinking of the great leaders in the struggle for African independence like Nkrumah, Nyerere or Kenyatta may have been, in their philosophy, as a reaction to this Western racism and cultural imperialism, there was marked stress on the value of autochthonous culture. However, they were very well aware that there was no way back: traditional patterns of culture seldom survived the colonial period unscathed, and moreover, when people like Nyerere opted for African socialism, simply out of economic necessity it was impossible not to take over values and elements (technology) from Western culture. *In the context of present-day Africa, acculturation therefore means the quest for new, integrated forms of society which overcome the deep split introduced into the African soul by colonialism and imperialism.*

The churches in Africa have a vital role to play in this process of acculturation. At any rate, it is in the sphere of religious experience that the above-mentioned split has manifested itself most powerfully. Desmond Tutu, the present Secretary-General of the South African Council of Churches, speaks of a religious schizophrenia under which the African Christian has suffered:

> With part of himself he has been compelled to pay lip service to Christianity as understood, expressed and preached by the white man. But with an ever greater part of himself, a part he has been often ashamed to acknowledge openly and which he has struggled to repress, he has felt that his Africanness was being violated. The white man's largely cerebral religion was hardly touching the depths of his African soul; he was being redeemed from sins he did not believe he had committed; he was being given answers, and often splendid answers, to questions he had not asked.

African theology is the attempt to look at this religious schizophrenia and, at least on a theoretical level, to transcend it.

A process of this kind is also characterized by a logic and dynamic of its own, and without a feeling for this specific pattern of development it is difficult to follow the course of African theology. Anyone who reflects on how long and how fundamentally the autonomy of the African has been undermined and trampled on by systematic contempt and mockery of his culture and religion will recognize the inevitability of a reaction which acknowledges the value of these traditions and even glorifies them. This reaction creates the necessary self-respect which is the indispensable condition for the search for a new liberating identity. Going back to old traditions and customs is therefore not a return to the fleshpots of Egypt but the necessary first phase of the difficult exodus from the slavery of Western religious and cultural domination.

The rehabilitation of traditional African experiences of reality (which are always religious) is an emancipation in itself, although in fact there is a danger of a reactionary shift when this search for authenticity is used ideologically in the interests of the new ruling class, which in many countries exercises dictatorial power. However, re-evaluation requires rediscovery, for the past is accessible only in a damaged, neglected form. Empirical investigation at a local level is necessary to connect the countless sayings, riddles, popular narratives, songs, prayers and dances with the experiences of life which they express. Oscar Bimwenyi of Zaire calls this, not inappropriately, the building of theology 'on the field of oral culture' (quoted by J.P.Heijke, in the Africa number of *Wereld en Zending*, 1981). Publications on this subject in recent years are not only almost too many to survey; they also produce such a kaleidoscopic picture that it is difficult to speak in general terms about *the* African religious sensibility or experience of reality.

However, there is a great need to speak in essentialist terms about *the* African experience and view of life. There is a tendency towards apologetic here: at any rate, distinguishing 'the nature' of African culture from that of other cultures must form the basis of the new self-respect. Clearly there is something like *the* African view of man, *the* African philosophy, and so on. In the title of the well-known book by John S.Mbiti (Kenya), *African Religions and Philosophy*, the word philosophy is deliberately put in the singular. The study by Placide Tempels, *Bantu Philosophy*, published in 1946, was of great significance in this respect. This Flemish Franciscan rejected the view that primitive peoples could have no ontology and no logic; however, he believed that they do lack the capacity to express this latent system of thought in adequate philosophical terms – and Tempels saw this as a task he was called to perform: 'The proof of a systematic development of Bantu ontology must be our work. And once it is done, we shall be able to tell the Bantu, and tell him clearly, what he thinks in his innermost heart about being. He will recognize himself in our words and reply: "You give us understanding, you know us perfectly, you 'know' as we 'know'".' The key concept which Tempels used to express the essence of the Bantu way of life was 'life-force', the force which permeates total reality and in which human beings share.

However much the paternalism of the Belgian missionary met the criticism which it deserves, we nevertheless find his insights, albeit in a more sophisticated form, once more in African investigators like Alexis Kagame (Ruanda) or Vincent Mulago (Zaire); and in any case many share the view that there is in fact no such thing as a specific African philosophy. More than was the case with Tempels, here strong emphasis is placed on anthropology: human life and human determination have a central place. Thus in the Final Communique of the Pan-African Conference of third-world theologians in Accra, Ghana, in 1977, African anthropology was mentioned as one of the sources of African theology.

For Africans there is unity and continuity between the destiny of human persons and the destiny of the cosmos. African anthropology and cosmology are optimistic. The victory of life in the human person is also the victory of life in the cosmos. The salvation of the human person in African theology is the salvation of the universe. In the mystery of incarnation Christ assumes the totality of the human and the totality of the cosmos.

The theologian and artist Engelbert Mveng, SJ (Cameroun), who certainly shared in the formulating of this text, points out emphatically that for African people the determinative feature of humanity lies in its involvement in the dramatic conflict between life and death, which becomes meaningful in the ultimate victory of life over death. Human life is the battlefield for the struggle between life and death, and human beings are combatants who opt for or against life. But here they do not stand alone; all that exists – spirits, cosmic forces, natural elements, living and dead human beings – is mobilized in this struggle.

Consistent with this basic view of humanity and the way in which it is determined are ideas like community and wholeness which African theologians and historians of religion constantly bring up, in apologetic or polemic, as a contrast to what they feel to be specifically Western. Thus the African sense of community is contrasted with Western individualism. According to Mveng, the individual is not a human *person* in the African meaning of the word; he or she is only an outline sketch which must be developed by integration into the world and society. The basic structure of the human person is a network of interpersonal and cosmic relations. People often point to the striking parallel with the social consciousness of early Israel, which finds its expression in the concept of 'corporate personality' introduced by Wheeler Robinson: the community represents the individual, just as, conversely, the individual embodies community. The deep-rooted feeling 'I am because we are, and because we are, I am' creates a clan solidarity which also embraces the dead and the unborn. As long as the names of dead ancestors are still known by the living, these belong to the community and their presence is revered. This attitude towards the living-dead (John S.Mbiti) has far-reaching consequences, say for land ownership; nothing is more disastrous than for people to be driven from the land, as happens within the framework of the 'homeland' policy of the South African government: 'The land provides them with the roots of existence, as well as binding them mystically to the departed. People walk on the graves of their forefathers, and it is feared that anything separating them from these ties will bring disaster to family and community life. To remove Africans by force from their land is an act of such great injustice that no foreigner can fathom it.' Thus Mbiti, and Mercy Amba Oduyoye recalls Kwame Nkrumah's remark, that 'land belongs to a vast family of which many are dead, few are living, and countless members are unborn'.

People are not isolated individuals, but form part of great associations which reach so far as to embrace the whole of creation. This sense of community is based on a holistic vision of life which African theologians contrast sharply with the Western dualism of body and soul, matter and spirit, secular and sacred. And it is this holistic experience of reality which is ultimately the legitimation for the argument for religion mentioned earlier. Over against the one-dimensional restrictions of Western culture, religion is promoted as the binding force in life: 'religion is a matter of taking each individual element as part of a whole, each limited feature as a representation of the infinite': these words from Schleiermacher's *Discourses on Religion* could aptly be applied here. Thus – to limit ourselves to one example – for Engelbert Mveng African art is essentially religious language and cosmic liturgy: 'In creating a new work of art the artist creates a new world and humanizes nature. Black African esthetics takes the cosmic battlefield where life and death confront each other and transforms it into the Elysian Fields where life chants its victory over death. Every work of art breathes a whiff of immortality into inert and mortal matter. Every rite, dance, piece of music, and work of plastic art is a cosmic celebration of life's victory over death. It is a cosmic liturgy.'

However, the apologetic ace of trumps is put on the table when African theologians argue that this holistic experience of reality and community are largely akin to the world of biblical narrative. In their view African spirituality is much closer to the Bible, and especially to the Old Testament, than the Christianity which has been imposed on Africans from outside, corrupted by individualism, dualism and secularism. Here they rightly point to the experience of numerous 'independent churches' which are still active in their thousands on the African continent. These usually small church groups – the Kimbanguists with their approximately four million members are an exception – which take their name from the fact that they avoid the sphere of influence of Western mission, have a striking preference for the Old Testament, which they use as a mirror of their own reality.

What is the explanation of this predilection for the Old Testament? In a clear account of 'Continuity and Discontinuity Between the Old Testament and African Life and Thought', included in the symposium *African Theology en Route*, Kwesi A.Dickson (Ghana) mentions three factors:
1. The detailed ordering and regulation of daily life offered by some books of the Old Testament corresponds to the predominant place occupied by the survival of ritual and other regulations in traditional African life; 2. The Old Testament speaks to people who are oppressed and humiliated – one thinks primarily of the central place occupied by Moses as liberator, political leader and lawgiver in the Zionist churches in southern Africa; 3. As in African tradition, so too in the Old Testament religion is not detached from the rest of life.

However, as Dickson says, there is a danger that the specific character of the covenant history of Israel and its God will be neglected, so that the element of discontinuity is not given its due. Is it possible to give full weight to the particularity of this history and yet speak of continuity? Dickson looks for an answer on three levels. *Theologically* one can speak of continuity because the *goyim* (nations) are also involved in the story of God with his people; the particularity of this history does not exclude its universal reference; God is also at work among the *goyim*. In *religious and cultural terms* there is continuity in that both in the Old Testament and in the African tradition, elements in nature – a fountain, an oak, the burning bush – can be holy places (however, the God of Israel is not a God of nature but creator of heaven and earth); and there is also continuity in connection with the above-mentioned sense of community (however, prophets like Amos and Deutero-Isaiah make it clear that the God of Israel is not a tribal or clan God but a God whose love transcends national boundaries). Finally, Dickson feels able to speak of hermeneutical or interpretative continuity because in the encounter with the Old Testament Africans cannot and may not leave behind their own questions and problems – however, here too it would be wrong to neglect the discontinuity, which lies in the fact that all the insights which both the Old Testament and African tradition have to offer stand under the judgment of what happened on Golgotha.

Incisive though this last comment may be in itself, sadly it remains a theological abstraction, because the author fails to explain why, and for whom precisely, the crucifixion of the Messiah represents a judgment. Perhaps this omission is connected with the fact that he does not go further into the phenomenon to which he himself draws attention, namely that many independent churches understand the Old Testament as a story of liberation from oppression and slavery (moreover the Nigerian Nathaniel I. Ndiokwere is concerned with this aspect in his detailed study of the role of the prophets in the African independent churches and biblical tradition, *Prophecy and Revolution*, London 1981). As is also the case with other representatives of African theology, Kwesi A.Dickson clearly has difficulty with the partisan character of the biblical narrative in favour of the poor and unprivileged; however, precisely at this point the critical questions of South African and Afro-American black theologians begin, since for them it is precisely this liberating reality of the Son of man which forms *the* great factor of continuity between biblical history and our present-day reality – a factor, moreover which does not derive its credibility from empirical and historical phenomena but from the actual commitment of faith.

The affinity between essential elements of their own tradition and the world of the Old Testament has led African theologians to take up the concept of the *praeparatio evangelica*: just as the Old Testament finds its fulfilment in Jesus Christ, so too traditional African religion can be understood as a preparation for the preaching of the gospel. The apologetic drift is clear. The message of Jesus Christ is not a rejection of pre-Christian religious experience. On the contrary, the fulfilment in Christ demonstrates how much the true knowledge of God was and is already present in African history and culture.

In the preceding paragraphs we have sought to make two things above all clear: 1. that acculturation is the basic problem of African theology; 2. that rehabilitation of one's own culture and history is a necessary first phase in the process of acculturation.

This last comment should not, however, make us blind to the fact that this first phase of the long road to a new, liberating identity is already beset with pitfalls. The difficulties encountered are above all of a methodological kind. One example is the use of the term *praeparatio evangelica*. It is not as innocent as it seems to bring this battered old rabbit out of the hat for yet another time. The term presupposes a schematic salvation-historical way of thinking which is based on the contrast between nature and grace, law and gospel, in which 'nature' and 'law' form a stage preceding the fullness of the gospel. The objection that must be made to this way of thinking is not just that the salvation-historical pattern is alien to the way in which history is told in the Bible from Genesis up to and including Revelation, but also that quantitatively, in terms of more and less, a rationalized 'Christian' knowledge of God is compared with 'natural' knowledge of God, this last being regarded as a human potential which finds its realization in Christianity. In whatever context, Christian theology completely goes off the rails when it loses itself in historical speculation about an alleged process of accumulative religious experience. Its theme is and remains the messianic reality of the resurrection event in which the last shall be first and the first last – and this reality cannot be dressed up in any kind of salvation-historical scheme.

However, the introduction of a notion like *praeparatio evangelica* is obvious and perhaps even unavoidable when the problem remains as it was described at the beginnig of this chapter in the quotation from E.Bolaji Idowu. The starting point of Idowu and other African theologians is the question of the correlation between two entities thought to be independent, the biblical and Christian tradition with its conception of God on the one hand and the African tradition on the other. Furthermore, the correlation discovered must, it is said, be worked out in a programme of what was formerly called indigenization and is now mostly described as adaptation or inculturation.

The great difficulty in this method of correlation – and *praeparatio evangelica* is an attempt to answer the question of correlation

– is that it implies a phenomenological comparison between two entities conceived of in static or essentialist terms: Christian tradition with its 'values' and 'elements' and African culture and history. Neither the pneumatological dynamics of the messianic kingdom nor the complexity and ambivalence of empirical history can, however, be done justice to in this way. The problem continues to revolve around the question how African creation myths, rites of initiation, ancestor worship, clan solidarity and so on can be adapted to or integrated into the Christian doctrinal tradition. Even where Western expressions of this tradition are relativized in order to make room for Africanization, a given interpretation of the Christian proclamation, not further open to rational discussion, remains the term of reference by which African religions and experiences must be tested – unless, as is the tendency with Gabriel M.Setiloane (South Africa), things are turned upside down and African traditional religion, in this case that of Sotho-Twana, is taken as the point of reference. In both cases the comparative method remains the one to be used, and this, as Charles Nyamiti (Tanzania) has rightly observed, stresses the positive elements in African religion at the expense of the negative ones – here one should recall the lack of freedom and the anxiety associated with tabus, or the exclusiveness of clan solidarity. Nyamiti argues for a broad approach which not only takes note of the whole context of history and culture but is also coupled with renewal in the sphere of the organization of theological training, liturgy and canon law (Nyamiti is a member of the Roman Catholic church). Although he uses the term, he does not, however, arrive at true contextualization, since whatever else, this presupposes two things which are missing in his account: a careful analysis of the contemporary social context of African theology and a recognition of the primacy of praxis (cf. Chapter 2 (a)).

Given what has been said above, it is not surprising that in past years there have been clashes between African theologians and representatives of Afro-American or South African black theology. In 1974 John S.Mbiti wrote an article in which he criticized black theology for its narrow focus on blackness and liberation. Fasholé-Luke (Sierra Leone) also thought that Christian theology had to transcend the political conflict and racial struggle, while Setiloane criticized the 'Western' character of black theology with its one-sided emphasis on political and economic problems at the expense of the cultural dimension.

However, for Desmond Tutu black theology and African theology are soulmates. Black theology has some lessons for African theologians, since hitherto these have contributed little to thinking about and solving the gigantic problems with which African countries wrestle. What does African theology have to say about the epidemic of coups d'état and military régimes, about development, poverty and sickness? Through its rehabili-ation of African culture and religion it has performed an important work of emancipation, but it has neglected its prophetic calling. Black theology reminds African theologians that this prophetic calling implies support for the poor and the oppressed.

Setiloane has dismissed Tutu's criticism far too easily by rejecting the appeal to 'prophetic calling' as a Western Christian cliché. When he concedes to Tutu that it is indeed high time that African theology 'should venture on the political terrain', the question arises why that has not happened so far or, if it has happened, why it has happened so seldom. As I indicated above, the answer to this question is connected above all with methodological presuppositions and starting points. At this point we have the real conflicts between black theology and African theology. Over recent years, however, a process of mutual rapprochement has without doubt got under way: on both sides there is a growing feeling that black theology and African theology are indeed soulmates, which can supplement and correct each other in their common focus on liberation from all slavery.

One important element in the development of African theology was without doubt the Pan-African conference of Third World theologians in Accra (Ghana) 1977. Although it is true that this conference organized by EATWOT represented only one particular trend among African theologians and is not to be identified with African theology as a whole, at the same time it marks a point of no return. It is significant that the theologians present in Accra could agree on the following programmatic passage in their Final Communique:

We believe that African theology must be understood in the context of African life and culture and the creative attempt of African peoples to shape a new future that is different from the colonial past and the neo-colonial present. The African situation requires a new theological methodology that is different from the approaches of the dominant theologies of the West. African theology must reject, therefore, the prefabricated ideas of North Atlantic theology by defining itself according to the struggles of the people in their resistance against the structures of domination. Our task as theologians is to create a theology that arises from and is accountable to African people.

Furthermore the declaration mentions three characteristics of such a new way of doing theology: (a) It is contextual, and in the context of present-day Africa this means that it is concerned with liberation from cultural captivity. (b) Because oppression is encountered not only in culture but also in political and economic structures and in the domination of the mass media, African theology must also be a theology of liberation, since the gospel of Jesus Christ requires involvement in the struggle to free people from all forms of dehumanization. (c) Special attention is required to the struggle against sexism, and this struggle begins at home, since, notwithstanding the prominent role that women have had in shaping African history, so far they have been excluded from theological work.

The characteristics mentioned are very important, not least because they give a clear perspective to all the work that has been done so far. Both the recognition of the inexhaustible arsenal of local oral tradition and attempts to systematize the specific African experience of reality along with the comparison between biblical or Christian features and elements from African tradition – all this material must be examined and tested critically, 'like a detective' (Ernst Bloch), to see whether it can be used as material in the process of acculturation: the creation of new forms of society in which the negative consequences of neo-colonialism and imperialism are overcome and the end of the exploitation of one person by another is in sight.

This last point might well be called utopian if we use the word utopia in the sense that it has for a thinker like Ernst Bloch. For him the cosmic and human reality itself has utopian connotations.

The incompleteness of the world makes history a process in which everything flows, everything is in movement. Longing is the source from which history wells up, and especially in religion we have a manifestation of this restless search for identity, for the fulfilment of the not-yet. So religion is not a finished affair; it is more than simply a reactionary bond to the fleshpots of Egypt; it too is also an expresion of utopia, of longing for the manifestation of the *homo absconditus*, the person who is still hidden.

If the ferment of the search for identity has begun anywhere, it is in darkest Africa, beneath the constantly expanding Sahara, where the traumatic experiences of colonialism and racism are still clearly to be felt. Paradoxically enough, the utopia does not lie buried under the rubble of past centuries. Despite everything, in present-day Africa there is a surplus of hope which still does not seem to have been eaten away by cynicism and scepticism. Of course the euphoria of independence from about 1960 is fundamentally over. The wickedness and vanity of military and civil potentates has seen to that, along with the enormous national burdens of debt, the corruption present almost everywhere, the immense suffering of millions of refugees and travelling workers, and the constantly increasing hunger and poverty in countries which are among the poorest in the world. Yet popular theatre, novels and poetry reflect not only this disillusionment but also the vital élan of an indomitable optimism which detects a radiant horizon behind the threatening clouds of the present.

The source of this love of life would have dried up just as quickly if it did not have deep roots in the soil of African culture and religion. African theology is therefore occupied in extremely necessary work when it tries to map out religious and cultural traditions. The positive value of this investigation into the past, however, turns into its opposite when the deep crisis of the present is left out of account. Africa, it is said all too often, is in a state of transition. African theology has its specific context, its *Sitz im Leben*, in this state of crisis and transition. It is important for its functioning that it should see this context with open eyes – otherwise it is anachronistically concerned with idealizing the past.

That means that social analysis must have a place alongside biblical reflection and investigation of African tradition. But analysis and the formation of theories is not enough by itself if contextualization is indeed concerned with liberation. The Accra Final Communique speaks of a theology which emerges from and is connected with the people. This last characteristic is impossible unless the people have a clear political choice – and so far that is too little recognized by the representatives of African theology (with a few exceptions). Involvement for the people is an empty cry if nothing is said about forms of oppression in whch a tiny upper class enriches itself at the expense of the people. But this bond is taken even less seriously if it does not lead to a positive and critical involvement in socialist experiments in which the people has a say about land, raw materials and means of production – even where, as in Mozambique or Congo-Brazza-ville, a Marxist-Leninist government sees church and religion as disruptive and retrogressive factors in the revolutionary process.

Special note should be taken of the fact that the Accra Communique mentions the independent churches as one of the sources of theology. This is a direct implication of the plea for a theology which 'emerges' from the people. If the subject of African theology must in fact be the people, and not an intellectual élite which has become uprooted and now wants to get back to the sources, then African theology must reflect critically to a far greater extent than hitherto on the spirituality and life-style of these usually local communities. (Here, of course, it must be pointed out that the difference between independent and estab-lished churches is becoming more blurred now that in many cases the latter are under African leadership and in them too the stress is beginning to be placed on a basic structure of small local communities.)

The spectacular growth of the independent churches is sympto-matic of the fact that Africa is in a phase of crisis and tradition, not only over the conditions of material existence and means of production, but also in religious and cultural terms. The statistics are telling: in 1900 7% of the African population was Christian, in 1960 30% and in 1978 45%. Now it can rightly be objected that the transition to Islam, to which, similarly, more than 40% of present-day Africans belong, or to Christianity does not in itself mean that people have broken with their original traditions. But that leaves the question of what makes people move so massively, especially to the independent churches.

J.G.Donders, lecturer in the University of Nairobi, has pointed out that the forming of ties with new communities is a typical African reaction in times of crisis and change: when Africans take the step of being baptized and thus initiated into the life of Jesus Christ, they do so in the expectation of finding a way towards solving everyday problems like sickness, lack of food, homelessness and so on: 'What the African has been and is concerned with is life here and now. A life that depends on God and on his ancestors, but which is also dependent on those who are still to be born. And it was only when it was understood that the old organization of life was endangered by all kinds of modern contacts and developments, that people began to look round for a new organization to belong to.'

Baptism and eucharist function as rites of passage which give access to the new community and the new life in Christ. This form of life, however, is not without problems. Faith healings, fundamentalism, intercessions, possession and speaking with tongues make critical Westerners suspect a thoroughgoing otherworldly faith which leaves social problems and relationships untouched. A political commitment backed by theory is usually lacking, while the exclusivism of the old clan solidarity lives on in the tendency to exclude other forms of being a church and to become sectarian.

Without losing sight of the negative aspects, we must note that appearances are deceptive. An other-worldly faith in the Western sense is alien to these African communities. There may be need and misery to excess in the African fields and on the African roads, but the earth is not seen as a vale of tears from which the tormented creature must be redeemed; far less is man regarded as a sinful individual who is in a bad way and can only share in eternal life through Christ's grace. In these churches, such an individualistic and dualistic view of life comes up against the African sense of community and a holistic experience of reality. At a time when upheaval has been great, especially in the cities, these local communities give people a new identity and security which embraces all aspects of life. 'They even organize within the liturgical context of worship the healing of the sick and the driving out of evil spirits like alcoholism, extravagance, antisocial behaviour and so on' (J.G.Donders). The Christ who is worshipped here is the Christ of Matthew 10.8, who said, 'Heal the sick, raise the dead, cleanse the lepers and drive out evil spirits.'

He is the healer and liberator who frees people from all these forces which stand in the way of a full realization of human life and human determination.

Just as in Latin American countries liberation theologians seek to function as 'organic intellectuals' (Gramsci) in Christian basic communities, so it is not inconceivable that academically trained African theologians will increasingly respond to the challenge of the countless African local church communities. These communities should then in a real sense be the setting for African theology. Here, though, the vital question is whether they can wield the divining rod by means of which it is possible to detect the liberating, ecumenical features at the expense of everything that binds people to the sacral power of Pharaohs old and new.

5

Theology in the Caribbean and the Rastafarian Movement

Franz Fanon, the psychiatrist and philosopher from Martinique, writes in his *The Wretched of the Earth*:

> The church in the colonies is the white people's church, the foreigner's church. She does not call the native to God's ways but to the ways of the white man, of the master, of the oppressor. And as we know, in this matter many are called but few chosen.

One can hardly speak more sharply, more one-sidedly than that. However, it was not Fanon's intention to give an objective, historically responsible view of mission. He shares an experience gained in the Caribbean and Africa 'one-sidedly', from the perspective of colonized men and women who have achieved awareness of their situation. This experience does not allow any premature qualification; first of all it must be understood and assimilated in its 'one-sidedness'. In his introduction to Fanon's book, which appeared in 1961, Jean-Paul Sartre said: 'Our victims know us by their scars and by their chains, and it is this that makes their evidence irrefutable.'

Fanon was driven to make his statement by his experience of the historical complicity of Christianity in creating a world divided into two, a Manichaean world in which the white skin of the colonist symbolizes freedom, goodness, knowledge, riches and power, and black is an expression of inferiority, passivity and ignorance.

In the Caribbean, which until the sixteenth century was a genuinely coherent entity populated by Indian people who had been living there for a long time, the rule of King Sugar and black slavery were the two factors which made this region the segmented society it still is. Characteristic of its Manichaean structure is the sometimes latent, sometimes open tension between the church communities from Europe and America with their specific theological background and the forms of religious expression among the victims of racism and colonialism. However varied may be the picture presented by Methodists, Lutherans, Herrnhutters or Roman Catholics in terms of church, society and theology, their church remains a church of the whites, of the ruling class – with all the attraction that this social status has for those who do not enjoy it. Even when missionary activities were undertaken by the black churches in America by people like George Liele and Moses Baker, who came to Jamaica in 1783, the system of slavery remained unaffected: the preaching of the gospel in Liele's black Baptist church required the explicit permission of the white masters. We are reminded of Fanon's words when, in the symposium *Troubling of the Waters* which he also edited, Idris Hamid calls God an outsider: 'Even the categories of our religious experiences are imported products which do not reflect our cultural and native experiences. We experience God as an outsider.'

Troubling of the Waters, which appeared in 1973, marks the beginning of an intense common search for a distinctive Caribbean theology. Since this stone was thrown in the pool the water has continued to be disturbed. Under the leadership of Idris Hamid, who died all too young, and while he lived was co-ordinator of the Caribbean Ecumenical Programme established on Trinidad, a process of theological collaboration came about which emphasized common study and reflection. Its constantly recurring theme is that identity is the basic problem of the Caribbean churches, and that this problem can only be solved (*a*) by a concern for regional unity and (*b*) by identification with the struggle of inferior groups and classes.

However, one cannot say that the profile of a new, specifically Caribbean, theology has already become clearer in the past ten years. Anyone who reads through collections like *Troubling of the Waters, Out of the Depths* (1977) or *Moving into Freedom* is likely to be weighed down, willy-nilly, by the impact of the almost montonous litany in which the charges against neo-colonial mission are constantly repeated. The negative element of criticism still predominates to such a degree that it is hardly possible to go on to the positive activity of the outlining of new forms. On the subject of a new vision of the missionary task of the church, most Caribbean theologians all too readily seek their salvation in Latin American liberation theology or black theology in America – and here too an identity crisis crops up! It is significant that the Caribbean area is still hardly represented in EATWOT.

This difficult state of affairs is not so surprising, though, when we reflect on the marked oppositions and the great differences in this region. It can be argued that the Caribbean contains in concentrated form all that may be said to be characteristic of the Third World as a whole. Colonialism, slavery, and contract work have seen that class conflicts have been bound up in a dense and complex way with racial oppression and sexism. As to the latter, it must be pointed out that women are still wholly absent from the collections of Caribbean theology mentioned above.

The immigration of new population groups from Africa, Europe and Asia, whether compulsory or not, has made this area a hotch-potch of cultures and religions – though there is still little evidence of collaboration and dialogue between churches and Hindu or Moslem organizations. Moreover, the struggle for identity and unity is complicated by the factor that the various countries are at different points on the time-scale of development: for example one could compare a socialist country like Cuba with neigh-bouring Haiti, where ninety per cent of the population is illiterate and every year thousands of people are sold as slaves to Dominican sugar-plantation owners – a fact which is all the sadder when we remember that this was once the scene of the glorious slave rebellion which in the view of Toussaint L'Ouverture, its brilliant leader, was to form the basis of a modern black nation with a modern economy focussed on the world market.

One consequence of the difference in time-scale mentioned above is that we can note that whereas elsewhere in the Caribbean the birth-pangs of a contextual theology are still very much in evidence, in Cuba, a strongly profiled distinctive theology has developed. This has its centre in the Seminario Evangélico de Theologia in Mantanzas, and Sergio Arce Martinez, Adolfo Ham and Raúl Fernandez Ceballos are its best known representatives.

This theology was expressed evocatively in the confession of faith accepted by the small Presbyterian church in Cuba in 1977. This confession has no claims on eternity, but is meant to express what the Christian community believes and confesses here and now, in Cuba in 1977. Because scripture is not concerned with eternal truths, but with revelation as history, this confession cannot and may not be other than a historically determined contextual event.

The Cuban confession embraces the Marxist-Leninist revolution in Cuba *con amore* and without eschatological reserve. This definition of status can only be seen in its proper historical perspective when we realize that the churches and their ministers occupied a privileged social position in the period before the revolution. Fidel Castro's seizure of power meant a break with this privileged position. Far from rejecting this *kenosis* of the church through revolution as an attack on Christian faith, the confession of faith sees this revolution as a process to which the church has contributed what is its real task in the world.

This task can be summed up in the word *diakonia*, service. However, the nature of this service on the part of the church, the body of Christ, cannot be other than that of God himself who became incarnate in man. According to the apostle Paul (Phil.2.7), Christ's *diakonia* is *kenosis*, emptying: he took the form of a slave, an oppressed person, in aid of humanizing men and women. 'Belief in Jesus Christ obliges the church to put humanity in the centre of its interests and to regard this humanity as a parameter for judging all things, in particular for evaluating its own doctrinal positions, the specific structures of the church and its special mission as church' (1.03).

The theology of the cross in Phil.2.7 calls for an ecclesiology of kenosis: the *diakonia* of the Son of man calls his community to a similar ministry. Very much along these lines, Adolfo Ham, in a contribution to *Out of the Depths*, relates Christ's threefold ministry – as priest, king, and prophet – to the church: 1. Its prophetic role implies an understanding of the revolutionary process, a theology of the proletariat, a rejection of the perverse solutions which are offered by capitalism, and the conscientization of the political action of Christians in a socialist society, beginning with the fact that the real prophet can never be a neutral observer but is always involved in the struggle for justice and love. 2. Through the priestly ministry the church develops its ministry as intercession and love, understanding prayer as pro-existence and love as militant solidarity with the oppressed, in order to make possible the reality of love among people. 3. Its royal ministry must be understood in terms of total service, in the same way as that of Jesus Christ.

Both in Ham's article and in the Cuban confession, all the emphasis is put on the fact that the church may not stand aside from the revolutionary process. Ham sharply attacked the notion that the task of the church should be to humanize socialist society and to create free places in Communist totalitarianism: 'What always emerges in this kind of approach is that under a capitalist régime, which is more unjust and less humane, such people never feel the direct call to reject the gods of capitalism, much less to want to humanize the system.' Adolfo Ham similarly rejects current church and theological thinking which, at any mention of the new man as the aim of revolution, stresses that according to the gospel the goal of history lies 'outside history'. Such a conception implies a historical pessimism which robs people of their expectations, in which any human struggle is doomed to failure from the beginning.

The Cuban confession of faith does not recognize any division of human history into a secular and a religious dimension: there is only one history, and this history is a history of salvation, because it is renewed by Christ from the underside, from the position of the oppressed. On the basis of Christ's incarnation, reconciling death and resurrection, God's kingdom is a real possibility within this history (and not, in a utopian fashion, beyond it). Without fear of being mistaken, the church may proclaim that beneath the socio-political and economic conflicts and controversies a development of indisputable and permanent value is taking place (cf. 4.B.01). Indeed, in this way the church gladly accepts the socialist revolution as a specific sign of the efficacy of God's kingdom. The Marxist-Leninist revolution has proved to be the only way of putting an end to underdevelopment (cf. 3.D.07).

Although the confession refrains from identifying the socialist revolution with God's kingdom in theological terms, unfortunately this theme is not developed politically. In his discussion of the confession of faith, Dick Boer has rightly pointed out that here the authors strikingly fall short of Lenin's insight in *State and Revolution* that the socialist state, too, needs to work for its own abolition. The fear of lapsing into the position of the critical outsider is clearly so great that though the new family code is welcomed as a contribution towards the establishment of a more just society, there is silence about the continuing practices of machismo, discrimination against homosexuals and white racism. This failure to note the contradictions of the revolution gives the appearance of uncritical solidarity, and this last is a contradiction in terms.

That is not to say that this confession is in fact little more than ecclesiastical approval of a socialist state system. In terms of biblical theology the confession offers often surprising perspectives. The theological insights of Barth, Hromadka and Bonhoeffer seem to have found their way to Cuba. The christocentric structure of Barth's *Dogmatics* influences the construction of the confession; Hromadka's view of the mission of the church in a socialist society has been an inspiration, and Bonhoeffer's comments on the 'non-religious interpretation of the Bible' and *disciplina arcana* are recognizable in a passage like this: 'The Reformed Presbyterian church in Cuba is aware that when it lives by this truth it comes dangerously close to radical secularization as this takes shape through God in Jesus Christ, and that it runs the same risks of incomprehension, suffering and crucifixion as those with which he felt himself to be faced' (5.02).

We can leave unanswered the question whether, as Bert Schuurman thinks, the Cuban confession has a triumphalist tone; but he is right when he points to the difference from Latin American liberation theology: if the Cuban confession speaks in a post-revolutionary situation, Latin American liberation theology has developed in a pre-revolutionary situation in which the prospect of radical change is often a very distant one. This difference in context means that there is much greater stress in liberation theology on the discipleship of Christ as identification with those who suffer. Liberation theology is also a 'theology of captivity'. Moreover, it looks for a specific Latin-American socialism and, unlike the Cubans, has reservations about the Marxist-Leninism which has developed in Europe; Marxism is gratefully accepted as an instrument for social analysis, but rejected in so far as it presents itself as a system with a world view.

Finally, a third distinction is that Latin American liberation theology has a Roman Catholic background, while Cuban theology in and around Matanzas has the stamp of the Reformation, with a stronger accent on biblical theology than we are used to from Gutiérrez and his followers.

The first beginnings of a common theological reflection on questions of unity and identity in the Caribbean as a whole are closely connected with the establishment of the Caribbean Council of Churches in 1973 at Kingston (Jamaica). The basis for this establishment was laid at the important conference on development in Trinidad in 1971, and this fact is a demonstration of the close connection in this region between church unity and development. Only when work is done simultaneously on both does the solution to the central problem of the distinctive identity of the Caribbean come a step closer.

The direction of the Caribbean Council of Churches is in agreement with this insight. The accent lies on 1. renewal of the church through training and the equipping of ministers and laity in connection with the search for forms of contextual theology; 2. projects of development in the sphere of agriculture, small industry, education and social training. It should also be mentioned that the Council, which has had twenty-nine member churches since the Third General Assembly in November 1981, publishes a splendid monthly, *Caribbean Contact*, which no one should ignore who wants to keep in touch with the social, political and church situation in the Caribbean.

Still, the work of renewal and development is subjected to heavy pressure from the past. The history of complicity in slavery and colonial exploitation cannot be undone. Outside the churches, the (West) African religious traditions which slaves and freemen, who in the colonial churches at best could take a place on the rearmost benches, brought with them in their compulsory crossing of the Atlantic ocean have helped them in their new situation. Voodoo in Haiti, Shango on Trinidad, Kumina and Pocomania on Jamaica, are forms of African religion mixed with Christian elements. The contract workers brought from Asia also revered their religious traditions, or created new forms like the Maldevidan cult, in which Hindu belief is fused with Roman Catholic elements.

Such forms of popular religion – which we understand to include the forms of religious organization of those whom Fanon called 'the wretched of the earth' – represent an enormous challenge to a Caribbean theology-in-the-making. Idris Hamid wrote in 1973:

> If we examine carefully the folk-wisdom that has arisen among the people we shall find in those practical wisdom sayings elements of a theology or philosophy of life that reflects our historical experience. Thus any attempt to arrive at a distinctive theology must examine the many 'non-church' ways in which the reality of God was communicated, experienced and expressed among the people. It would seem that God had to do a lot of his work underground.

The folk wisdom to which Hamid refers is above all the skill and the resourcefulness to survive under extreme, humiliating circumstances. It is a matter of recognizing God's underground ways in the complicated textures of the counter-culture which the black slaves were able to weave and which went underground to the degree that it escaped the white authorities.

The Rastafarian movement, which thanks to the reggae music of Bob Marley, Peter Tosh and so many others is at the moment very much in the limelight, is rooted in the underground survival culture of Jamaica's black slaves, who never accepted their lot. In Rasta belief, which emerged in the 1930s among black people who, despite the abolition of slavery in 1834, were still marked by poverty, humiliation and repression, we find the continuation of the spirit of the proud maroons, the escaped slaves who built a society of their own in the protection of the hills and from there harassed their white masters. This belief maintains the subversive recollection of the constant rebellion of slaves, of the rebellions under the leadership of the Baptist preachers Sam Sharpe (1831) and Paul Bogle (1865). Rasta Bob Marley sings their story, in the distinctive language of the Rastafarians, in his 'Redemption Song', which is included on his 1980 LP *Uprising*.

In the history of Jamaica one figure stands out who more than anyone else is the direct forerunner of the Rastas. This is Marcus Garvey, maligned by some as a charlatan but revered by the

Rastas as a prophet of black liberation. He laid the religious and philosophical foundations on which the Rastafarian movement could develop.

Marcus Moziah Garvey, born in 1887 in St Ann's Bay, Jamaica, founded the Universal Negro Improvement Association (UNIA) in 1914 which after his arrival in the United States in 1916 he succeeded in developing into the largest black organization that has ever existed. In 1919 the number of members totalled more than two million. Garvey's slogan was, 'Africa for the Africans at home and abroad'. Garvey succeed in giving people who still bore the deep scars of slavery a feeling of self-esteem and pride about their African origin. 'Africa' functioned as a religious symbol of a glorious past and a hopeful future. The steamboat company Black Star Line, on which Garvey was literally to suffer shipwreck, symbolized the longing for repatriation. Found guilty of financial malpractices, Garvey spent two years in prison before being exiled to Jamaica in 1927. There he founded the People's Political Party and without much success fought for Jamaican self-government, the introduction of minimum pay, land reform and so on; in 1935 he moved his headquarters to London where he vainly sought to build up a School of African Philosophy. He died in 1940.

Although Garvey knew that 'God has no colour', he thought that because white people imagine God as white, black people equally have the right to see God through black spectacles: 'We Negroes believe in the God of Ethiopia, the eternal God – God the Son, God the Holy Spirit, the God of all times. This is the God in whom we believe, but we shall worship him through the spectacles of Ethiopia.' The subtle ambivalence between nationalism and universalism expressed in these words is characteristic of Garvey's thought and action. We find the same ambivalence in the Rastafarian movement, in which some groups, like the commune of Prince Edward Emmanual's Ethiopian National Congress, believe in black supremacy in a very explicit way, while others, like The Twelve Tribes of Israel, put the stress on racial equality and tolerance.

On his departure from Jamaica in 1919 Marcus Garvey seems to have spoken of the coronation of a black king from Africa who would bring redemption. When in November 1930 Ras Tafari Makonnen was crowned Emperor of Ethiopia, took the name

Haile Selassie and received titles like 'King of Kings', 'Lord of Lords' and 'Conquering Lion of the Tribe of Judah', some people thought that Garvey's prophecy had been fulfilled. Half-educated, unemployed black people in the difficult crisis period of the 1930s saw the new emperor of distant Ethiopia as their redeemer. In the slums of Kingston the Authorized Version of the Bible was consulted and proof texts were found for the divinity of Haile Selassie in Rev.2.2-5: 'Weep not; behold, the lion of the Tribe of Judah, the root of David, hath prevailed to open the book, and to loose the seven seals thereof.' Psalm 68.31 also spoke clearly to believers: 'Princes shall come out of Egypt, and Ethiopia shall stretch forth her hands unto God', as did passages like Ezek.37.19; Rev.19.16.

Despite persecution and intimidation from the authorities and the police, the Rasta community grew. Repatriation to Ethiopia was a fiercely cherished expectation, and groups did in fact travel to the promised land. However, in recent years a change can be detected and the stress is now placed more on mental repatriation. The death of the Emperor in August 1975 was of course a critical time for the Rastas, but it could not basically shake their faith. The spiritual presence of their black Messiah remains present in all that they do.

Leonard E.Barrett has described the Rastas as a messianist-millenarian cult – messianist because of their belief in the person of Haile Selassie, and millenarian because of the expectation of an imminently good future on earth. Although such a religious historical labelling may not be intrinsically incorrect, it does not tell us much about the decisive question how Rasta belief functions, whether it liberates or alienates.

Any understanding of Rastafari depends on the degree of understanding of the significance of racism and colonialism for their victims. Racism not only justifies economic exploitation, but implies the total rejection of the manhood of the other, the black person. Racism and colonialism (neo-colonialism) preserve a Manichaean world in which, as we heard from Fanon, a black skin symbolizes inhumanity and bestiality. The Rasta belief reproduces and reflects this Manichaean division of the world between black and white, but the other way round. The world of the black, the world of Africa, is human. By contrast, Western capitalist and imperialist civilization, in which there is no prospect for the blacks, is inhuman.

The culture, and in particular the economic and political system of Jamaica, is identified with biblical Babylon, the land of captivity. Babylon stands for the whole complex of attitudes which humiliate the black man and hold him captive: the capital of Babylon is Rome, which was responsible for the execution of Jesus, which waged war on the black Hannibal, which allowed Mussolini's troops to invade the Ethiopia of Haile Selassie, and which above all is the place from which the Pope sends his lies into the world; moreover, the Rastas are very well aware of the specific involvement of England in the black slave trade: Queen Elizabeth I and her reincarnation Elizabeth II are seen as the personification of the whore of Babylon.

Set over against Babylon is Ethiopia, the biblical name for Africa. Ethiopia is Zion, the place of salvation. Africa/Ethiopia is the promised land, heaven. For the Rasta heaven is not the hereafter but a specific place on earth. The return of black people from the Diaspora to Africa is, however, the moment of universal remigration, when the surviving remnant of every people will return to the land of its origin and the Indians, too, will again take possession of Jamaica (here we have an expression of the universalist tendency of Rasta belief).

This transformation of the Manichaean world picture brought about by the dominant system of 'Babylon' is the result of a pattern of belief which emerges from the depths of slavery and racism. The dialectic of this conversion is ultimately none other than the dialectic of which Sartre speaks in his analysis of *négritude*, when he says: 'because the black, more than any other, has suffered from capitalist exploitation, more than any other he knows the meaning of rebellion and love of freedom. And because he is the most oppressed, he necessarily strives for the freedom of all when he works for his own liberation.'

The Rasta expresses his repudiation and rejection of the dominant ideology as the ideology of rulers by a way of life characterized by great individual freedom and mistrust of authoritarian leadership. Differences between Rastas are numerous, but that does not alter the fact that there one can talk in terms of a common life-style which breaks with the dominant culture and makes room for the experience of personal identity. The famous dreadlocks, the long uncombed hair, are for many Rastas the outward sign of their religious calling: like the Nazirites in biblical times, they are set apart by their God. Moreover the use of ganja (marijuana) has a religious and healing (also in the sense of medicinal) significance. By contrast, Rastas abstain from alcohol, cigarettes, coffee and related products of the Western consumer society; by preference they eat I-tal food, natural, vegetarian food. However their most successful incursion into the white structure of cultural domination is the specific Rasta language: the Rastas enriched Jamaican creole, always regarded as a mark of social degradation, with countless new expressions and grammatical constructions, and elevated it to be the mark of their own identity and self-awareness.

One striking linguistic innovation is their use of the word I. Joseph Owens relates in his book *Dread* that the Rastas consistently avoid the word 'me', which is used in Jamaican creole wherever the first person singular might be expected: 'Me have me book'. The Rastas still feel that this expresses the subjection of the slave, the way in which the slave is treated as an object. By using I instead of me and my the Rasta stresses the fact that he is the subject of his own history.

The plural 'we' is replaced by 'I and I', which symbolizes both individual freedom and the unity of the Rasta community, based on the unity with Jah, God.

The first syllables of particular keywords are also replaced by I (I-tal instead of vital; I-ration instad of creation; I-tection instead of protection). This expresses a special bond with these terms.

According to Rasta belief, the restoration of the original Africa and the ultimate universal repatriation will be preceded by an apocalyptic time of blood, fire and brimstone, when nature takes vengeance on all those who transgress her laws. Although this last judgment is already in prospect, the fulfilment of history cannot be forced. Most Rastas patiently wait in meditation and discussion for what is to come: here their way of life and vocabulary function as a barrier and protection against the Babylon system which is still dominant.

By contrast, others are more militant, but among them, too, there is no clearly delineated political strategy of liberation. The mistrust of politics is deeply rooted. The Manichaean view of the world has its effect here: political and social changes *within* the existing system do not lead to real justice and peace. When Rastafari is called a liberation movement it is not because it has a clearly articulated political and economic programme for social change but because it creates room alongside the existing system for people to experience mental and physical liberation from a slave's existence (and that in itself is powerful enough).

But that is not the whole story. We must go still further and ask ourselves why among the Rastas religious and artistic imagination (poetry, reggae, sculpture) has so much the upper hand over sober political and strategic thinking. Why do marginalized black people in Jamaica and elsewhere not oppose their exploitation in the same way as, for example, the European (white) proletariat have done? Here we come up against the problem of the specific dynamics of the race struggle as compared to the class struggle, which are directly connected with the Manichaean division between white and black introduced by the slave owners and colonists, and with the associated, unsuccessful attempts at the total annihilation of black people's humanity. Black slaves, male and female, have not, however, allowed themselves to be degraded so that they become objects without a will of their own; they have always felt the contradiction between their social and legal status as things (objects, possessions) and their destiny as human beings. This contradiction has given birth to the belief in which blackness is itself a pointer to true humanity.

We find this belief again among the Rastas. However, given the perseverance of the power of the Babylon system, dialectical change and renewal in the Manichaean view of the world is always related to the ultimate reality, which the Rasta anticipates in the workings of his imagination. In the sound of reggae and the reading of Rasta poetry this last reality, Jah (God), is evoked and experienced. Africa lives in language and music – a world which is yet to come. The Africa/Ethiopia which the Rasta celebrates is an imaginary continent, the product of an anticipatory imagination which refuses to accept Babylon as the ultimate reality.

'Africa' is a specific utopia which can also become a reality on Jamaica, and therefore among the Rastas it is increasingly being said that physical repatriation to Africa is undesirable; these people think that the liberation must take place on Jamaica and in the Caribbean itself. Therefore, we venture to suppose, we must not overestimate the significance of Haile Selassie as a historical figure. The historical appearance of this hardly enlightened despot was a point of contact for the expresion of a belief which has much deeper historical roots: that blackness, this stumbling block, points to God's humanity, which is expressed in his partisan love for the poor. This partisan love is expressed in a moving way in 'So Jah Seh', on the LP *Natty Dread* by Bob Marley and The Wailers.

For years the churches have been indifferent to the Rastafarian movement and have ignored it. However, in more recent times we can detect a clear change of direction. Within the Caribbean Council of Churches and kindred organizations there is a tendency to regard the movement as a praxis of liberation, and the thought of the Rastas as at least an implicit form of black liberation theology. We might ask whether Rastafari is not here being put prematurely within a Christian theological framework.

We find another approach in the excellent report by the English Catholic Commission for Racial Justice (*Notes and Reports*, No. 10, 1982). This argues that the Rastafarian movement should be seen as a full non-Christian religion. One of the recommendations of this report reads: 'Christians and Christian churches must seize and encourage any opportunity to make contacts with the Rastas, as they would with believers of any other non-Christian religion. For example, the Rastas often have nowhere to meet: Christian churches should allow them to use their buildings.'

Although the Rastas continue to reject established Christianity, we can also note important shifts on their side. According to recent accounts a group like The Twelve Tribes welcomes young, middle-class whites, accepts the Bible as a whole and rejects earlier interpretations of some parts of the Authorized (King James) Version. At the moment it is hard to say where this development will ultimately lead.

Latin American Liberation Theology

As we saw earlier, most of the forms of liberation theology being discussed in this book usually arose almost contemporaneously and independently of one another. However, public opinion associates the term liberation theology primarily with Latin America. Incorrect though it may be, the misunderstanding is understandable in itself. It is an unmistakeable fact that the Latin American theologians have been foremost in recognizing and describing the decisive methodological and hermeneutical implications of this new way of doing theology. Gustavo Gutiérrez' *Theology of Liberation* met with world-wide recognition, however much it was written with an eye to the Latin American situation. Latin American viewpoints come well to the fore in the Final Declaration of the first EATWOT Conference in Dar-es-Salaam (1976), a key passage from which I quoted in Chapter 2. They include commitment as the first act of theology and the rejection of any academic theology divorced from action, viewpoints which we find again in Gutiérrez, Míguez Bonino and Assmann. The brothers and sisters from other continents have increasingly appropriated the methodological insights of this Latin American theology – though it should also be added that from the beginning there has been opposition within EATWOT to the dominant position of Latin American theology and its analysis of society.

What was said in Chapter 2 about theology as critical reflection on a praxis of liberation is the hallmark of Latin American theology. In fact we should discuss yet again, here, the methodological and hermeneutical decisions which are involved in such a concept of theology. However, to spare ourselves space and the reader trouble, we do not want to be repetitive, and will content ourselves with referring specifically to what was said in the sections (*a*) A new way of doing theology and (*b*) Break and continuity there.

Another of the essential insights of Latin American theology is that any text belongs in a specific context and may not be abstracted from it. That of course is also true of the texts of Latin American theologians themselves. So we shall first look, however generally, at the specific situation in Latin American church and society, as the liberation theologians experience it and interpret it. Then we shall try to indicate what this situation means for thought about Christ (christology) and the church (ecclesiology). To end the chapter we shall touch on some critical questions which have been put to the Latin American theologians in the framework of the EATWOT discussion.

(*a*) The discovery of dependence

Riobamba is a provincial city in Central Ecuador. The place is part of the diocese of Leonidas Proaño, who has been bishop here since 1954. Proaño, who prefers to wear a tattered Indian poncho, is the gentle embodiment of what in itself is a pretentious claim, 'the option for the poor' to which the Latin American bishops committed themselves at their Third General Assembly in 1979. As a follower of Mahatma Gandhi, and thus without responding to violence (structural violence) with violence, Leonidas Proaño has dedicated himself to the lifelong task of being in the literal sense a beast of burden for maltreated Indians. Without letting himself be intimidated by the opposition, which often takes the form of the brute violence of knuckle-dusters, or the hostility of the landowners, he and his fellow workers have supervised the establishment of agricultural cooperatives and schools, and they have succeeded in giving the oppressed, subjected Indians of this area a feeling of their own worth, making it increasingly possible for them to organize their own exploitation.

Near to Riobamba, Proaño has built a retreat house in a simple style which, as Penny Lernoux relates in her book *Cry of the People*, is intended to be as unintimidating as possible to Indians who have never slept in a bed or stood under a shower. However, one day in August 1976 a police bus arrived at this house. The

Ministry for Internal Affairs had ordered the soldiers in it to arrest all those present in the Santa Crux house and take them to the capital, Quito. That happened. And so, quite unexpectedly, a distinguished collection of bishops, nuns and theologians, who were in the house for a five-day international conference on pastoral affairs, were put in the bus at pistols and machine-gun point.

When they arrived in Quito, the members of the conference were put in prison. Only Leonidas Proaño was taken for interrogation. In vain officials of the government tried to get a confession from him that there was subversive literature in the house, like books by Trotsky and Camilo Torres: 'The only subversive document at the conference,' replied Proaño, 'is the Bible.'

Of course this stupid occurrence, which led to the expulsion of the thirty-seven foreigners, did not go unnoticed. Never before had so large a number of bishops been subjected to the humiliation and intimidation which ordinary mortals in Latin America so often endure. The incident could be dismissed as a clumsy manoeuvre of a government which hardly had a reputation for scoring highly in intelligent action, were it not that there was every occasion for supposing deeper motives. The then Secretary General of the Council of Latin American Bishops (CELAM), Mgr Alfonso López Trujillo, rightly spoke of a 'well-planned campaign against the church'.

It should, though, be pointed out that this Colombian priest was described, with some justification, by a group of priests on the occasion of his nomination as cardinal in February 1983 as 'the most sophisticated disciple of Machiavelli who ever infiltrated the church of Jesus Christ.' At any rate, when he made this pronouncement López Trujillo was hardly in a position to make criticisms of others. Directly, or through his associate Roger Vekemans, he had excellent relations with the CIA, and this organization had extensive dossiers on 'subversive' priests, laity, bishops and liberation theologians. These dossiers served as the basis for a well co-ordinated campaign against the church by a number of régimes which propagated the ideology of National Security and the 'war against Communism'. The incident in Riobamba was part of this 'well-planned campaign against the church', which got under way in 1975.

The strategy of this attack was to aim neither at the church as such nor at the clergy as a whole. It was a question of 1. weakening the internal divisions within the church; 2. threatening progressive church leaders or putting them under suspicion by secretly circulating Marxist literature where they were working; 3. arresting foreign priests who espoused the cause of the poor or encouraging their expulsion from the country by playing on nationalistic feelings.

The action against the church, in which at least ten military régimes were involved, was not unexpected. While the list of martyrs which Penny Lernoux has included in her book shows that the period 1975-1977 is a black spot in the death and martryrdom of church officials, it also demonstrates that the persecution of 'subversive elements' in the church began in 1969/1970. Wherever groups of Christians, priests and laity, work for liberation, i.e. for the implementation of and respect for the most elementary human rights which are withheld from two-thirds of the population of Latin America, they meet with intimidation, suspicion or worse. What makes this commitment to liberation so threatening in the eyes of the leading classes is that it cannot be dismissed as the particular initiative of a few radical priests or religious. Since the Second General Assembly of the Latin American Episcopate in Medellin (Colombia) in 1968, work for 'a comprehensive, bold, urgent and radical change and renewal' has been official church policy. These discussions marked a turning point in attitudes to the wretchedness and oppression of the Latin American people. Since Medellin in 1968, to use the terminology of the CIA, the church has become 'vulnerable to subversive penetration'.

Without doubt Medellin was able to build on the renewal of Vatican II (1962-1963). However, the assembly demonstrated that it had a voice of its own by showing that the specific reality of the Latin American subcontinent was the starting point for its thought. Terms like 'dependence', 'domination' and 'the imperialism of multi-national finance' were used to describe the situation in Latin America. This state of affairs was described as social sin, as it is in conflict with the will of God 'who, in the fullness of time, sends his Son in the flesh, so that he might come to liberate all men from *all* slavery to which sin has subjected them: hunger, misery, oppression and ignorance, in a word, that injustice and hatred which have their origin in human selfishness.' This image of a liberating God who does not will peace without justice also determined thinking on the question of violence, which in fact was the central problem at Medellin. The bishops condemned violence as something which is in conflict with the gospel, but the violence that they had in mind here was primarily that of oppressive structures and mechanisms.

The interesting thing about Medellin is that the Assembly in some respects marks the transition to a new approach to the reality of Latin America which took place at the end of the 1960s and which we shall later meet in a more developed form in the theology of liberation. On the one hand Medellin is still clearly indebted to the technocratic idea of development (*desarrollismo*) dominant in the 1960s which begins from the division between 'developed' and 'underdeveloped' countries; here the approach and achievements of the developed countries are the model for the government needed in underdeveloped countries. On the other hand, the use of terms like 'dependence' and 'domination' points to a new understanding of the reality of Latin America in which thinking is no longer in terms of development and underdevelopment, but the fundamental opposition is expressed by the terms development and *liberation*.

It must not be imagined that the bishops assembled in Medellin suddenly became revolutionary Marxists, far less is there cause to suspect that they were excessively sympathetic towards the guerrilla war of Che Guevara or the decision of the Colombian priest Camilo Torres to devote himself wholly to the political struggle and, later, to guerrilla warfare. But those among them who succeeded in making their mark at the meeting had seen and experienced enough of the Latin American situation in their pastoral practice to know that only revolutionary change could put an end to the blatant poverty and exploitation. They knew of the unrest, the political awareness and the longing for liberation among *campesinos* and industrial workers; they were familiar with Paulo Freire's popular pedagogy and work of conscientiz- ation; and although the church hierarchy was traditionally anti- Communist, it recognized that the capitalist world economy was at least as great an evil as Communism. As early as 1966, in one of the preparatory documents for Medellin, Helder Camara, who had direct experience of the harsh military dictatorship in Brazil after the coup in 1964, condemned the 'internal colonialism' of the ruling order as 'collective sin'.

It is worth realizing that figures like Helder Camara and Leonidas Proaño did not discover the fact of Latin American dependence in libraries, by economic and sociological theories and analyses, but by going about their pastoral work among the people. However, the empirical evidence of this dependence calls for theoretical clarification of the underlying causes and connections; otherwise it remains caught up in subjective experiences which can be told but cannot be rationally argued and explained.

This analysis of structures of dependence appeared in the 1960s, and it is known as the 'dependence theory'. However, it is quite wrong to assume that since Medellin a number of bishops and priests, along with kindred liberation theologians, clergy untrained in social and economic matters, have succumbed to a Marxist theory of society which hardly goes further than propagating the breaking of ties with the capitalist world. This conception fails to see what precedes the susceptibility towards the dependence theory: the discovery of the *contradiction* between the *de facto* dependence and domination, there for anyone to note with ears to hear and eyes to see, and the myths of development and progress. Gutiérrez is right in saying that the use of the 'dependence theory' by liberation theologians cannot in fact be called naive because there is no alternative. However, it is no more than an expedient for understanding reality. As soon as better means are available, it can be replaced.

The term 'dependence theory' causes misunderstandings. There is no such thing as the dependence theory, nor has there ever been. Of course, since the failure of technocratic models of development became increasingly evident in the second half of the 1960s, Latin American economists and sociologists have made intensive studies of structures of dependence which determine what has been happening in the economics, politics and ideology of the various Latin American countries. Despite their diversity in aim and results, these analyses have been given the label 'dependence theory'. This designation is misleading in that it suggests a homogeneity which in fact is not present and cannot be present, because the contexts of the individual Latin American countries are too divergent for it.

Of course these analyses of the subordination of Latin America to the capitalist system in general and the United States in particular together represent the first coherent attempt to see the Latin American reality from a Latin American and not a Western perspective. They are opposed to two approaches which, remarkably enough, are more alike than might be thought possible at first sight. (*a*) They criticize theories of development which begin from a structural dualism between traditional and modern society; in this view underdevelopment is caused by backwardness (economic, technological or cultural). A well-known example of the theory is the book which President Kennedy inspired for his Alliance for Progress, W.W.Rostow's *The Stages of Economic Growth: A Non-Communist Manifesto*; however, in its plan for development (e.g. as the basis of the programme of the Frei Christian Democrat government in Chile), the Economic Commission for Latin America (ECLA) also began from a structural dualism between a traditional and a modern sector, which was said to be the cause of economic stagnation and social inequality. (*b*) The orthodox Marxist theory of the Communist parties in Latin America orientated on the Soviet Union was also criticized because in fact it too works with a structural dualism between traditional-feudal and bourgeois-industrial society; in its view, the bourgeois need to be in power in feudal agrarian society and a process of industrialization must have taken place before the objective conditions are present for the revolution of the proletariat.

The dependence theory opposes this structural dualism with the view that development and underdevelopment are two sides of one and the same capitalist process of development. The first to develop this view, perhaps far too schematically, was André Gunder Frank in his study *Capitalism and Under-development in Latin America. Historical Studies of Chile and Brazil*. Frank speaks of 'development of underdevelopment'. In his view conquest by the *conquistadores* brought Latin America within the sphere of expanding mercantile capitalism, and from then on the sub-continent was allotted a peripheral role – on a periphery which is structurally dependent on a centre which determines both the economic and class structure and the culture of the Latin American countries.

In general, the dependence theory distinguishes three forms of dependence in the history of Latin America. 1. The first phase, which lasted till about 1930, is that of the primary export model; the economic organization of the Latin American countries was directed towards the production and export of raw materials, and the importation of industrial products; the expansion of the share in exports hampered industrialization and was even less favourable towards other forms of economic activity. 2. The second phase was directly connected with the international economic crisis of the 1930s; this crisis meant an export crisis for Latin American countries, and led to a process of a substitute import industry of lighter industrial products. 3. The third phase has been characterized by the internationaliz- ation of the home market: the continuation of the process of industrialization calls for an accumulation of capital and a technological know-how which can only be realized by a combination of domestic capital with multi-national capital: the familiar example of this associated pattern of development is of course Brazil, but the present-day bewilderingly high burden of debt in that country shows how difficult it is to restructure this dependent capitalism.

It is obvious that the analysis of economic, political and ideological structures of dependence and domination and their interconnection can never be completed. Those prone to speak of *the* dependence theory should note that since the first publications of Frank, F.Cardoso, E.Faletto, T.dos Santos, R.M.Marini and others, it has progressed a long way and has also found support outside the Latin American sub-continent. In addition to the analysis of external relationships of dependence it has also become concerned about the internal structures of dependence in Latin American countries and the active role of the national middleclass (associated with multi-national enterprises) in maintaining the social domination of the oppressed classes.

At the congress on 'Liberation and Christian Faith in Latin America and the Netherlands' held in May 1979, Gonzalo Arroyo discussed the question whether the dependence theory can be a valid tool for liberation theology. In his positive answer he produced two specific arguments: first of all, he pointed out that in principle the dependence theory seeks to give a comprehensive interpretation of the Latin American reality from the viewpoint of the oppressed class (although here he points out that hitherto it has not been completely successful because its anthropological and cultural analysis is not sufficiently developed and its class analysis is too traditional and pays no attention to popular religion); his second argument was that by its (critical) use of Marxist terms of reference the dependence theory establishes a relationship between intellectual analysis and militant action on behalf of farm-workers, workers and Indians.

Here are in fact the two most important points of contact between dependence theory and liberation theology. It must also be added that liberation theologians have not taken over already completed social analyses to use in their own work in a naive and uncritical way, but have also themselves made important contributions, whether as individuals or through collaboration in interdisciplinary groups. One example of the former is the study by the Belgian priest and theologian Joseph Comblin of the ideology of National Security (*Le Pouvoir Militaire en Amérique Latine. L'idéologie de la Sécurité Nationale*, Paris 1977 – this book is dedicated to Leonidas Proaño!); an example of the latter is the congress, held in Costa Rica in 1978, of sociologists, political theorists, economists and theologians on the activities and ideology of the Trilateral Commission, the group formed in 1973 which tries to co-ordinate and defend the three great centres of power in the world: North America, Europe and Japan (see H.Assmann (ed.), *Carter y la lógica del imperialismo*, Costa Rica 1979, two volumes). Moreover, in this connection the bitter fact should not be forgotten that a considerable number of representatives of both liberation theology and dependence theory have to live temporarily or permanently in prison – which is a considerable handicap for their work (and not just for that).

Just as Medellin in fact implies the recognition of the 'discovery of dependence', so it has given a green light to the praxis of liberation among the rising basic communities which are also referred to as *Iglesia popular*, the people's church or the church of the poor (in this connection one can understand all three terms, 'poor', 'oppressed' and 'people' as renderings of the biblical *anawim*: as such they are almost synonymous).

The term 'liberation theology' was not yet current in 1968. Granted, Gustavo Gutiérrez gave a lecture with the evocative title 'Towards a Liberation Theology' in July of that year, but his book *Theology of Liberation* was only to appear three years later, in 1971. It was the first systematic reflection on the *already existing* commitment to liberation to appear in print. So when Gutiérrez speaks of this commitment as the primary element and as theology as the 'second step' which follows, this methodological insight is not a speculative principle but an accurate reproduction of the actual course of events. Here, of course, one can also ask the question, as José Míguez Bonino was to do later, whether all theology, even where that is not intended, is not a 'second action' which follows a social commitment that is not put into words and explicated.

The way in which Gutiérrez relativizes theology in principle is not simply a matter of method but is fully determined by the content of his theology: 'To paraphrase a well-known text of Pascal, we can say that all the political theologies, the theologies of hope, of revolution, and of liberation, are not worth one act of genuine solidarity with exploited social classes.' The elements of liberation in human history, however incomplete and fragmentary they may be, are significant as salvation history; they are provisional, proclamatory ways of mediating the kingdom of God proclaimed by and embodied in Jesus Christ. Here Gutiérrez resolutely rejects any division between salvation history and secular history, or between history and eschatology. In no way may theology legitimate a praxis which represents a flight from daily reality; salvation history as the history of God's actions is no abstract timeless process to be located in a sphere beyond the reality in which we live, but this history is – despite everything, despite massive wretchedness or the so predictable logic of unjust power relationships – the place where salvation comes about. Gutiérrez, with his thorough knowledge of church history and the history of theology, knows the current theological views about salvation history and world history, but that does not move him from the basic position that in essence there is only one history, namely the history which finds its determination in Jesus Christ, whose work of redemption embraces all dimensions of human existence and brings it to its complete fulfilment; and that means that human history is in essentials salvation history.

If we understand Gutiérrez aright, then he maintains on the one hand that all is created, all is redeemed in Christ (cf. Col.1.15-20), and on the other that people are present in this history (of salvation) not as passive objects but as subjects, called to 'make' this history. People always realize their own humanity through work (cf. Gen.1.28), by breaking with conditions of slavery (cf. the story of the exodus), by building a society of justice. The eschatology of the kingdom of God and the history of human relationships, behaviour and decisions are dialectically related. The kingdom of God does not end in human revolutions, and liberation in Christ may not be reduced to political liberation. But on the other hand God's kingdom is at the same time present in the experiences of human liberation: 'the liberating action of Christ – made man in this history and not in a history marginal to the real life of man – is at the heart of the historical current of humanity; the struggle for a just society is in its own right very much a part of salvation history.'

From this it becomes clear why for Gutiérrez involvement in what he calls 'the praxis of historical liberation' is of vital importance. In theology this commitment comes first; without this commitment theology withers and loses its vitality, because it lacks the source from which it needs to draw. Scripture, too, remains a dead letter if it is not read in a community of men and women which has committed itself in this way. The 'historical praxis of liberation' in which the Christian community is involved is the only basis on which the reading of scripture and the analysis of social reality can be fruitfully related to each other.

However, one cannot speak of theology without speaking of the theologian. This is what Gutiérrez himself said in the speech which he gave in Nijmegen in 1979 on the occasion of his honorary doctorate:

It is well known that in the making of liberation theology the theology comes 'afterwards', is a second act. First it is necessary to commit oneself to the historical praxis of liberation and to the proclamation of the Word on which it is focussed. But this does not mean that the theologian only emerges in the second activity. The presence of the theologian in what we call the first activity is a necessary condition of his or her thought. What comes second is the theology, not the theologian. Within this context the theologian must be an 'organic intellectual' (I borrow this term from Gramsci), i.e. must have an organic connection with the popular movement for liberation and with the Christian communities who practice their faith at its grass roots. Sometimes this involvement entails the risk of physical death, and always it entails the death of the wisdom of the wise. So we could say that talk about a first and second element is not simply a question of theological method but rather a question of life-style, a way of confessing faith. Finally it is a question of spirituality, in the strong sense of the word. Put more precisely: our method is our spirituality.

In Latin American countries there has long been a close connection between church and state: the state provides the church with numerous aids and privileges and in exchange for that the church legitimizes existing power relationships. Although this model of the 'Spanish dream' became critical when political independence from Spain and Portugal came about, in the 1930s a new positive relationship developed with the (populist) power of the state which was termed the 'new Christian society'. When Gustavo Gutiérrez and his followers oppose this association with the power of the state and its allied ruling class by means of the 'historical process of liberation' and thus opt for another link between the church and the oppressed classes, then there is a very real danger that this new alliance may prove to be the mirror image of the old: that the Constantinianism of the right will be then opposed by a Constantinianism of the left and Christ as the heavenly monarch who sanctions the existing order will be opposed by Christ the revolutionary.

Precisely in order to escape this danger of religious messianism, Gutiérrez maintains the dialectical relationship between history and eschatology; any event of a revolutionary kind has a provisional character and may not be baptized as Christian in any way. Gutiérrez and his followers now associate this dogmatic insight, which is common enough in the European theology influenced by Karl Barth, with the conviction that it is also necessary to give methodological form in theological discourse to this dialectical tension between history and eschatology. This method implies that the Bible is not related directly to the Latin American reality without historical mediation – the Bible does not function as a recipe book or as a legitimation for political standpoints – but that it is assigned a place of its own in the analysis of social reality.

In this way any generalized, impressionistic talk about present-day reality is banished from theology – and on this point the Latin American theologians put critical questions to the Western European 'political theology' of Johann Baptist Metz and Jürgen Moltmann. If Christian faith is related to historical and social reality in its totality and thus is not pre-eminently an intrinsic existential event; if, moreover, this historical reality presents itself above all in the histories of the powerful, then a theology which seeks to identify itself with the struggle of the poor must find room for a social and analytical intervention which is in a position to unmask the myths of the powerful and demonstrate the structures and mechanisms of exploitation and dependence which underlie them. The need for this intervention, without which liberation theology cannot be 'critical reflection on historical action' (Gutiérrez), has led it to replace Aristotle with Marx.

Of course this last sentence needs qualification. However, in its excessive simplicity it does say something of real importance. The Aristotelian categories form the ingredients of traditional, scholastic Catholic theology, which is based on the scheme of nature and supernature (grace). We can argue over the question whether and how far this theology is the reflection of the feudal mediaeval structures within which it came to flourish. But at all events it remains an interpretation of the world from the perspective of revealed truth. For a theology which wants to do justice to the dynamic of God's kingdom as an eschatological reality in history, it is inadequate.

Therefore it looks for a social and analytical approach which does not just interpret the world but realizes that the important thing is to change it. So Latin American theologians turn to Marx, who formulated the thesis that 'The philosophers have only interpreted the world in various ways; the important thing is to change it.'

How do the insights developed by Marx and later Marxist

theoreticians (Gramsci, Althusser) affect Latin American theology? It has already been said often enough that Marxism does not function here as the framework for a world view but is used critically, in full awareness that this theory, too, has its historical connotations. Very schematically, we can distinguish three elements in the help Marxist theory offers to liberation theologians. 1. In the so-called 'dependence theory', Marxist theory provides an instrument for analysing the class conflict in the social formations on the Latin American sub-continent. 2. The conception of theology as critical reflection on a praxis of liberation contains underlying Marxist insights into relationship of theory and practice. 3. Along with Freud, Marx is the 'master of suspicion', as Míguez Bonino put it, following the French philosopher Paul Ricoeur: the suspicion that the leading ideas could be the ideas of the leaders gives rise to a hermeneutical approach which Míguez Bonino describes as follows: 'Every interpretation of the texts which is offered to us (whether as exegesis or as systematic or as ethical interpretation) must be investigated in relation to the praxis out of which it comes... Very concretely, we cannot receive the theological interpretation coming from the rich world without suspecting it and, therefore, asking what kind of praxis it supports, reflects, or legitimizes.'

To sum up, we conclude that Latin American liberation theology stands or falls by its methodological and hermeneutical starting points and presuppositions. There are four chief elements in its methodology which, while together they form one indivisible process, must clearly be distinguished from one another. First comes commitment; a second distinctive element is social analysis; the re-reading of biblical stories and church pronouncements from the perspective of the oppressed classes occupies a very important place; and finally, people return to the actual situation, where the results of biblical study and social analysis are related with an eye to pastoral practice and politics.

(b) Christology in captivity

The question must be asked whether Gutiérrez and his *companeros* did not attach too much importance to the 'historical praxis of liberation' at the end of the 1960s. In the 1970s the perspective became bleak. The military dictatorships spread over the sub-continent, and the picture of the 'new man' evoked by Che Guevara was smeared in blood. With economic, political and ideological support from the United States, and covered in the rear by an ideology of National Security which claimed to be defending the values of Christian civilization, the military mercilessly eliminated any opposition. The coups of Pinochet (Chile, 1976) and Videla (Argentine, 1976) were accompanied by countless acts of torture and murder. Although in a number of countries, above all Brazil, there was talk of a prudent policy of *apertura*, of openness to the limited form of democracy which was thought desirable by Carter and the Trilateral Commission, this new situation did not make the struggle against dependence and domination any easier. If one thing has become clear, it is that the 'historical process of liberation' has meant martyrdom, captivity and death for countless men and women. This praxis demands a high price. And if the revolution is finally successful, as in Nicaragua in 1979, the hardest thing – the building of a new society – seems yet to come!

In the past ten years, the church, too, seems to have paid the price of the struggle for liberation: at least a thousand priests and religious have been martyred. And the *Iglesia popular* has been under attack not only from outside but also from within. In 1972, after the CELAM assembly in Sucre (Bolivia), under the leadership of Secretary General López Trujillo there was a planned campaign on the part of the conservative sector of the episcopate to do nothing about the results of Medellin and to condemn liberation theology. From outside Latin America, especially from the bishops and theologians of West Germany, there was fierce opposition to liberation theology. The action centred on the preparations for the third General Assembly of Latin American bishops, which was to take place in Puebla in 1979. We know that the stratagems of López Trujillo failed and that the episcopate went so far as to declare a 'preference' for the poor. But that did not come about without compromise. What happened at Puebla brought clearly to light the fact that the Catholic Church in Latin America has two faces: in addition to the *Iglesia popular* – powerfully supported, above all in Brazil, by the episcopate – the strictly hierarchical church is also growing, with its old ideal of the 'new

Christian soceity'. The end of the confrontation between these two models of the church is not yet in sight.

The traces of all these developments can be found clearly enough in the publications of liberation theologians. Although liberation remains the basic framework, there are other accents. Above all the Brazilian theologians, at work in a country which from as early as 1964 had experience of a harsh dictatorship and repression, began to talk in the 1970s of a 'theology of captivity'. Spanish-speaking theologians also realize that a rapid change is imminent and that while the avant-garde of the 1960s had great powers of imagination, they did not know how to convey their vision to the people and took too little account of the *de facto* economic and ideological power relationships and mechanisms of oppression.

In a contribution to the collection *Frontiers of Theology in Latin America*, the Brazilian theologian Leonardo Boff wrote: 'We today live in a situation of captivity. To believe and hope and work for liberation in such a situation, when we are fairly sure that we will not live to see the fruits of our work, is to incarnate in our own day the cross of Christ.' The quotation says a great deal. Boff maintains the primacy of the work of liberation, the 'historical praxis of liberation'. But this work is done in a utopian hope which extends beyond the bounds of direct verification. This hope involves suffering, since its protest against suffering and injustice makes it dangerous in the eyes of the authorities, and as a result it provokes new repression, new suffering. At the same time, however, 'the suffering implied in hope can generate awesome and unexpected forces for liberation'. In this last statement Boff says something that is becoming increasingly central for Latin American theologians: the dialectical relationship between suffering and liberation, between cross and resurrection.

It was Leonardo Boff, and Jon Sobrino working in El Salvador, who, in 1972 and 1976 respectively, wrote christological studies in which the Latin American context and the experiences of Christian basic communities in situations of massive oppression form the explicit framework of reference.

For both authors, the answer to the question who Jesus is is always contextual; in other words, it is always connected with the specific situation in which the question arises. The situation – one need only think of El Salvador – is characterized by unbelievable suffering. However, one does not gain access to the reality of the life, death and resurrection of Jesus Christ by transcending the situation but only by accepting this suffering and, if necessary, martyrdom as a consequence of commitment to love, freedom and justice. True knowledge of Christ and God is only possible by actually following the way of Jesus. Specific discipleship is the locale of christology.

Connected with this last insight is the fact that strong emphasis comes to lie on the historical character of christological reflection. Christological dogmas cannot be understood without following the historical course of their formulation. Liberation theology is allergic to any trace of docetism (i.e. the doctrine that God only assumed a phantom body in Christ); it wants to take seriously the fact that Jesus was truly man. In the Preface to the English edition of his christology Sobrino says: 'If the *end* of Christology is to profess that Jesus is the Christ, its *starting point* is the affirmation that this Christ is the Jesus of history.'

At any rate in its first phase, christology is Jesuology. Without 'the historical praxis of Jesus', actual discipleship is impossible, and this in turn is the condition of true christological knowledge. Thus the hermeneutical circle is complete.

This Jesuology must prevent christology from being what it often has been in history: an instrument in the hands of the powerful, for whom the death and resurrection of Christ form a religious and metaphysical event without political and social implications. For liberation theologians, Jesus' crucifixion is the consequence not of a supernatural destiny but of a life in the service of justice. They continually stress that Jesus led his life in an insignificant place on the periphery of the Roman empire which had a surprising likeness to the present situation in Latin America. The death of Jesus is the logical consequence of his option for the poor in the midst of a people suffering under extreme exploitation and dependence. Traditional christology starts from the fact that Christ died for all men to redeem them from their sins, but in this way it loses sight of the fact that his death was the direct consequence of a *sinful* situation and that Jesus' proclamation of the coming of the kingdom of God can be understood only against this background.

Sobrino especially has tried to show that the centre of Jesus' life lay outside himself: his life was not determined by 'God' as a general concept, a universal explanation, but by the kingdom of God. This kingdom means the fulfilment of the Torah, the Law of Moses. Jesus stands in the prophetic tradition of the Old Testament and his activity can be understood only in that light. In his historical reconstruction of the life of Jesus Sobrino thinks that he can demonstrate a marked growth and development in Jesus' awareness of his own calling. Jesus' eschatological proclamation, 'The time is fulfilled and the kingdom is at hand. Repent and believe in the gospel' (Mark 1.15), still falls wholly within the framework of the orthodox tradition, though it is a radical version of it. However, Sobrino thinks – though on doubtful exegetical grounds – that this proclamation led to a crisis, the 'crisis in Galilee' (cf. Mark 8; Matt.13), which brought about a break in Jesus' awareness of his relationship to the kingdom of God. His belief in the kingdom undergoes a radical change which means that he surrenders all that he has – his life, his ideas and even his conception of God: 'After the crisis in Galilee Jesus went to meet an unknown future over which he had no control.' For Sobrino, the paradox of the life of Jesus lies in the fact that in the last phase of his life in the service of justice he was in ignorance of the coming of the Day of the Lord and the future of his own mission, but nevertheless entrusted himself fully to God the Father, who was to abandon him on the cross.

The crucifixion represents a complete break with any theodicy, with any natural conception of God. There is no continuity between the abandonment of Jesus by God on the cross and God's presence in the resurrection event. It is impossible to speak about God in one word – monotheistically; we can only speak of God as Father, Son and Holy Spirit. Here Sobrino has borrowed a good deal from Jürgen Moltmann, who in his book *The Crucified God* tries to show that the reality of cross and resurrection makes both a theistic and an atheistic concept of God impossible. However, whereas in Moltmann we get the impression that in the last instance the whole of human history, in a Hegelian idealistic sense, is taken up into the trinitarian event, in Sobrino, one might almost say historically and materialistically, the contradiction between the absence and presence of God in cross and resurrection is connected with the contradictions in human history and with the 'sinful situation' which Jesus faced in his life. The relationship between Father and Son is a relationship which is mediated historically: 'One can say that Jesus becomes the Son of God rather than that he is simply the Son of God.'

This last statement has great theological implications. By becoming the Son of God, Jesus reveals to us the way of the Son, the way by which anyone becomes Son of God. 'Thus Jesus does not reveal the absolute mystery' – he lets God be God, as Sobrino says elsewhere, but, 'He reveals how someone can respond to the absolute mystery by trusting in an obedience to the mission of the kingdom.' In this sense Sobrino argues for a rehabilitation of the New Testament category of firstborn: as firstborn Jesus stands in a relationship of Son to the Father, but also of brother to other human beings. This last point is stressed considerably when in an article by him in *Concilium* (1982, no.3) we read that in a situation of oppression like that in El Salvador one first of all believes in the Son of God because of the likeness there is between a crucified people and the Son of God as suffering servant. In the New Testament the title 'servant of God' (*pais Theou*) is used here and there, but it later fell into disuse. The designation goes back to the prophecy of Deutero-Isaiah, but it is exegetically difficult to discover whether the suffering servant of the Lord relates to an individual, a group – the remnant of Israel – or the people as a whole. The quotation Sobrino makes from a sermon by Mgr Oscar Romero in 1979 is important here: 'In Christ we meet the type of the liberator, the man who is so identified with the people that biblical exegetes can no longer distinguish whether the Servant of Yahweh proclaimed by Isaiah is the suffering people or Christ come to redeem us.' With this suffering people Romero – and Sobrino with him – is thinking of the people of El Salvador for whom he has pastoral responsibility. The mutilated and tortured people makes up 'what is lacking in the suffering of Christ' (Col.1.24), and here Sobrino again quotes the murdered archbishop, who at Corpus Christi could say: 'It is most opportune to pay homage to the Body and Blood of the Son of Man while there are so many outrages to his body and blood among us. I should like to join this homage of our faith to the presence of the Body and Blood of Christ, which we have shed, with all the blood shed, and the corpses piled up, here in our own land and throughout the world.'

With theologians like Sobrino and Boff one can talk of an operational, in other words a historicized and politicized, mysticism of the cross. There is a mystical *communio*, community, between the crucified people (wherever and in whatever period of history that may be) and the crucified God who himself has undergone the terrors of this world. However, at the same time the crucified people preserves the mystery of the Trinity by holding fast to the hope of the kingdom and continuing the struggle for liberation from all slavery. 'A crucified people that at one and the same time upholds the liberator God of the Exodus and the God of the cross, is stating that it believes in God and what it means by that God in whom it believes', as Sobrino puts it.

From this it becomes crystal clear yet again that the primacy of the 'historical praxis of liberation', affirmed by Latin American theology, is more than a hermeneutical and methodological question. This involvement in the historical processes of human liberation is no less than cognitive access to the mystery of savation. In these processes God's kingdom is made concrete and manifest, albeit in a provisional way. Therefore they are more than parables of or references to the kingdom and the work of redemption that takes place in Christ. Without identifying human elements of liberation with the kingdom, the theologians of liberation are at the same time inclined to see these elements as its historical embodiment.

This last point was clarified in the following way in the Final Document of the Fourth Congress of EATWOT (São Paulo 1980): 'To help us understand the relationship between the Kingdom and historical liberations we might use the analogy of the mystery of the Incarnation. Just as in one and the same Jesus Christ the divine and the human presence each maintain their identities, without being absorbed or confused, so too is the eschatological reality of the Kingdom and historical liberations.'

The methodological decision for the primacy of the praxis of liberation thus rests on the theological presupposition that God's kingdom, though eschatological in character and never exhausted in history, cannot establish itself without historical mediation: therefore the 'historical praxis of liberation' is an essential, albeit transitional, contribution to the building of the kingdom.

(c) Basic communities and popular religion

The praxis for which and within which liberation theology seeks to function has increasingly clearly, over the 1970s, become that of the Christian basic communities, so it is not surprising that the EATWOT Congress in São Paulo had as its theme 'The Ecclesiology of Basic Christian Communities'. These small communities, of which there are more than 50,000 in Brazil, form the setting for liberation theology. They are the context for theological reflection in three respects: 1. as the 'historical praxis of liberation' which precedes theology; 2. as a source of ecclesiology; 3. as places where the poor 'break through' in history.

1. The Christian basic communities form part of the people's movement and popular opposition in Latin America: they form the framework within which, as the Final Document from São Paulo puts it, 'the people finds a space for resistance, struggle, and hope in the face of domination. There the poor celebrate their faith in Christ the Liberator and discover the political dimension of love.'

The phenomenon of the basic communities is very complex, and there is no question of being able to do justice to it in a few lines. Moreover, much more empirical investigation is needed if we are to obtain anything like a complete picture. Basic communities emerge in the country and on the periphery of the great cities. They owe their origin to a variety of factors, including the great shortage of priests, the need to encourage the participation of the laity, and the desire for a distinctive, Latin American form of the church. However, the resolve to come together regularly as a group can also be the direct consequence of social resistance, for example to the confiscation of the land or the threat of the destruction of a shanty town.

There is no reason to idealize their existence. Inevitably these cells, which often must grow in the face of oppression in the most literal sense, are confronted with countless difficulties. Being a member of a basic community often involves great personal risk. There are areas in Central America where groups have been massacred simply because they owned a Bible; anyone with this book was regarded as a terrorist or a Communist – in the eyes of the authorities the two things were synonymous. So in the north of Guatemala there are groups who bury the Bible in the ground after their weekly meetings.

However, even when we have considered this new development with all due sobriety, there is no disguising the fact that the assembly of bishops in Puebla was right in regarding the pheno- menon of Christian basic communities as a 'reason for joy and hope for the church'. For all the differences in the stages of their individual development, they in fact constitute a new form of being the church: the church of the poor. The word 'basic' does not primarily denote people who do not belong to the church hierarchy – although a pyramidal church structure thinning towards the authorities at the top and with a broad basis of 'ordinary' believers is at the same time in conflict with the way in which people experience themselves as people of God; the most important thing is the social significance of the term 'basis': the majority of the members of this community are 'ordinary', i.e. in the Latin American context, marginalized people.

It is important to note that, contrary to the desires of some church authorities, the Christian basic communities do not form a third way, as a specifically Christian alternative to capitalism and socialism. These nuclei are not organizations parallel to the people's movement, but are an integral part of it. Their members are involved in the people's movement and 'seek to live their faith and break bread together in such communities' (Gutiérrez). Their cell-like structure, formed by a small number of people who share the same dwelling or place of work, makes possible a *koinonia* (community) which, measured in social terms, comes close to authentic democracy, i.e. they jointly bear responsibility for social and political action. It is this democratic commitment which is experienced as a threat by a ruling class which pleads that it is defending the values of free, democratic Western society by eliminating this danger!

At the same time, this *koinonia* means that the question of the significance of the Word of God for the present situation is not left to the individual conscience but is the subject of common reflection. However vulnerable, the basic communities are already a partially liberated zone in which 'ordinary' people can be themselves, in which all join together in reading the Bible, analysing the situation and developing and implementing a political strategy. Word and reality, action and meditation, liturgical celebration and political action are not detached, but interrelated and held together by the group as such, operating as a collective subject.

This last feature has important implications for doing theology. If the basic communities are themselves the 'historical praxis', the first stage which is prior to the stage of theological reflection, that does not mean that this reflection is suddenly left to some academically trained theologians, who take the trouble to instruct the basic communities. The groups as a whole, *ecclesia* in the full sense of the word, continue to remain the *subject* here. However, the collective theological work is far from making the contribution of the professional theologian superfluous. He or she may be dethroned as an autonomous academic subject, but as an 'organic intellectual' he or she is a welcome and indispensable ally.

We can see from *The Gospel in Solentiname*, by Ernesto Cardenal, and from the writings of the Dutch Carmelite Carlos Mesters, who is at work in Brazil, what happens when a group of men and women who are clearly aware of their marginal position in society reads the Bible together. This is clearly a 'political reading' of the Bible! The illiterate farm-workers and labourers bring with them their experiences of helplessness, suffering, of a world full of conflict and opposition between rich and poor, when they enter the world of biblical stories. The surprising discovery that they make here is that the reality of the biblical narratives is in fact their reality. They discover the Bible as a book which in fact belongs to them, the poor, but has been estranged from them by clergy who have allied themselves with the ruling class. Carlos Mesters writes: 'In the past we members of the clergy expropriated the Bible and got a monopoly in its interpretation. We took the Bible out of the hands of the common people, locked it with a key and then threw the key away. But the people have found the key and are beginning again to read the Bible. And they are using the only tool they have at hand: their own lives, experiences, and struggles.'

The professional theologian only dispenses with one function when he (and alas it is almost always 'he'; female theologians are still rare in Latin America) is completely at the service of the group, takes its popular culture seriously and tries to learn from the experiences of the people with whom he is dealing.

Someone who has thought and written a good deal about the

way in which theory and practice are connected in the life of the basic communities in a process of 'hermeneutic meditation' is Clodovis Boff, the younger brother of Leonardo. Himself an active member of a basic community, he describes this process in an article for *Concilium* (1981, no.144) in the following words:

In the first place, the reflection of the basic communities always starts from reality, from questions raised by the members of the community. There is no theologizing from academic questions, or those in vogue. On this level, the community is helped by some 'organic intellectual' (Gramsci) such as a social scientist, and in the absence of such, by its own professional theologian. This is what the methodology of theology in Latin America calls 'socio-analytical mediation'.

Then, the social situation analysed is compared with the Word of God. Here, there are two 'sub-moments' to consider. First, they try to understand the meaning of the text, and here the services of the theologian, or an exegete, are most helpful. Second, on the basis of the first, or textual, meaning, they go on to find an actual, or 'actualized' meaning, relating to the situation under discussion. Here the community naturally works collectively. The methodological approach that ensures the proper process of this operation is called 'hermeneutic meditation'.

Finally, they return to the present situation, but now in the light of the indications thrown up by the confrontation between the situation analysed and the gospel reflected on. This is 'practical meditation' (pastoral or political). So it will be seen that the process of reflecting on faith, that is, the theology of the groups, is wholly inspired by a practical purpose: *agape*. This is where theology reaches its term, only to begin again at once, as life begins again.

These last words of Clodovis Boff make it clear once again that the 'historical praxis of liberation', here summed up in the word love (*agape*), is a process which constantly continues, begins over and over again. But however fragmentary and broken the realization of the *agape* may seem to be, it may nevertheless be regarded as a specific historical mediation of God's kingdom on earth. In fact, as I have already argued, this last feature is the great theological presupposition which underlies the methodology of Latin American liberation theology.

2. The church is the community which is called to give form to the historical mediation of God's kingdom and make *agape* visible. The converse is also true: where this *agape* becomes reality, God's people is formed. At least according to the Second Vatican Council, the church is the *sacramentum* of God's purposes for the world, and the Latin American theologians interpret this to mean that the church makes visible the saving meaning of Jesus Christ and his mission in the world by serving as a sacramental sign and a sacramental instrument of liberation.

However, the world in which the church makes grace and the kingdom of God tangible is not a global, undifferentiated entity which ecclesiology can happily deal with in general terms. The world of Latin America is a class society, torn apart by oppositions and conflicts. The church does not stand above or outside these conflicts, but is called to be a sacrament in a society based on class. However, anyone who does not remember that the church itself is also a product of society is guilty of a dangerous form of idealism. Here Latin American theologians put forward serious criticisms of the current ecclesiological approach among European theologians. Taking the ecclesiological studies of Hans Küng as an example, they give the impression that the church exists in and through itself and disregard the fact that as it is, the church is always limited and determined (though not in a determinist way) by the socio-political and economic history of society with its specific means of production (thus especially Leonardo Boff). This omission enables them to evade the complex problem of how the theological truth of the church as the sacrament of God's plan and the body of Christ can be reconciled with the sociological fact that the church cannot in any way avoid the contrasts and conflicts of the society of which it forms a part.

Making use of the conceptual framework provided by A. Gramsci, Boff argues that in a class society there is always a ruling class which constantly works for the consolidation of its power by imposing its conceptions of reality on the lower classes and thus achieving an ideological consensus. It tries to enmesh the church in this struggle for hegemony, and the concept of 'Christian society' or 'the new Christian society' is the result of this connection between the institutional church and state power.

However, the hegemony of such a 'historical bloc' is never total. The oppressed classes in turn appeal to the church in their struggle to free themselves from the yoke under which they suffer. The church is therefore unavoidably an arena in which the class struggle is fought out. It can function to strengthen the hegemonic block, but it can also fulfil a revolutionary function.

For Boff, the phenomenon of Christian basic communities is the manifestation of a church which has definitively broken with the '(new) Christian society'. It is the breakthrough of a church which is bound up with the oppressed classes. As such, these communities form a new church, but not a church which differs from that of the apostles and of tradition. This is a church which, in its service to the poor, draws the ecclesiological consequences of Phil.2.7, the 'kenosis' of the Messiah Jesus. The mission of the Son, who has taken the form of a slave, determines the mission of the church which incarnates itself among the humiliated and the downtrodden.

Church authorities find it difficult to approve of this new reality, and that is not surprising, since in fact it represents a break with a situation in which the religious monopoly of knowledge and power rests with an élite of ministers and theologians. In their church-political strategy the authorities are therefore concerned above all to find a place for the basic communities within existing hierarchical structures. Their concern is for the unity of the church – conceived of in uniform and static terms. By contrast, for liberation theologians unity is structured round the mission of the church. Mission and apostolate are a task for the whole church: not only an ordained élite of ministers but the ecclesia as a whole is apostolic. The basic communities are not cut off from the one Catholic church. They have no difficulties with the existing parochial church stucture. They break with the perversion which calls itself Christian society, not with the institutional church: 'They have the same faith, they administer and receive the same sacraments, and they are in communion with the larger church and its hierarchical structure. But this interior unity is created and nurtured by reference to something outside: i.e., the church's mission' (Boff). This missionary task, which gives form and structure to unity, is the realization of the 'preference for the poor' (Puebla) and the *diakonia* of a new society which is more in accord with the gospel of liberation and reconciliation.

3. Since the beginning of the 1970s Latin American theology has undergone a marked development. It is not easy to sum up this development under a single heading. But we would probably not be far wrong to describe it as a process in which the poor increasingly become the subject of theological thought rather than its collective object.

Underlying the origin of liberation theology is an experience which can be described as the discovery of the world of the poor. The absence of this world from prevalent theological thought necessitated the 'epistemological break'. Initially, the prime emphasis was on the need for a radical commitment towards this world; the world itself remained in darkness as the sphere of exploitation and alienation, where the 'culture of silence' (Paulo Freire) prevailed. In fact the poor remained the people without culture and history, the great unknown.

However, especially in Brazil, other voices could be heard, though these were initially drowned by the Spanish-speaking theologians. The 'culture of silence' is an expression which brings together these two apparently exclusive concepts; the very combination of the two terms expresses very accurately the ambivalence of popular culture, in which experiential wisdom and deep alienation are both present and intertwined in a complex way. Gradually more attention was paid to the challenging, liberating side of popular culture and the religion in which this culture is steeped. This piety is not just an expression of the oppression and misery of the people, but is also protest; it is in fact the 'sigh of the oppressed creature, the courage to face a heartless world, as it is the spirit in spiritless circumstances' (Karl Marx). The close connection between oppression and religious experience is expressed quite blatantly in some areas, where the commemoration of the crucifixion on Good Friday unleashes powerful emotions and people identify not only spiritually but also physically with Jesus' suffering; however, the feast of the resurrection, of Easter, is not celebrated...

In the eyes of liberation theologians the *comunidades cristianas de base* are places where popular religion is 'cut'. If on the one hand the belief of the poor functions as a source of energy for their daily struggle, on the other hand Bible study and social analysis are necessary elements in liberating the religious experience from alienation. However, this dilution of religion in the service of liberating praxis is not a matter for professional theologians but is done by the group itself in a permanent process of reflection and action. The poor themselves are the ones with the initiative, and they have it because they, the wretched of the earth, are the people of God. Here we come upon a very important point which is stressed increasingly strongly in the thought of liberation theologians: 'It is the poor who are the natural vehicles of the utopia of God's kingdom' (Leonardo Boff).

After the Second Vatican Council and the inspiring Medellin conference, many priests and theologians turned to the work of 'proclaiming the good news to the poor' and being 'the voice of the voiceless'. Then, however, according to Gustavo Gutiérrez, came the irruption of the poor, their irresistible invasion of the history of the Latin American sub-continent. Although in the past the poor have never accepted their lot in a completely passive way, this irruption, with its terrible cost in terms of human life, is the great fact of recent Latin American history and forms the *de facto* background and cause of the events which come into world news. Gutiérrez says: 'This fact gave us deeper insight into the whole matter of evangelization. Working in the midst of the poor, exploited people, whom we were supposedly going to evangelize, we came to realize that we were being evangelized by them... This fact is coming to dominate our work and our view of the church. Experience has shown us that it is the poor who are doing the work of evangelization. We are coming to realize in a new way that God is revealed in history and that God is revealed through the poor.'

However, in our view it is precisely at this point that we find the real stumbling block which Latin American liberation theology puts in the way of European theologians, especially Protestants. Are the poor not romanticized here in a manner which is politically naive and theologically irresponsible? Moreover, have not Karl Barth, K.H.Miskotte and H.Gollwitzer shown that it is possible and necessary to confess the God revealed in Jesus Christ as the partisan of the poor without in so doing lapsing into a natural theology which promotes the poor to being mediators of revelation?

Precisely because the theology of Barth and that of the liberation theologians have so much in common – the rejection of the 'Christian society', the combination of theory and praxis (dogmatics and ethics), the primacy of reality above possibility in theological epistemology – a conversation between the Latin American theologians and those who see Barth's theology as the great breakthrough in the history of modern theology could be fruitful. Any discussion, however, is doomed to failure from the start if no attention is paid to the difference in context and experience which underlies the two.

It is nonsense to suppose that through Barth's criticism of experience (internalized and privatized) as the basis for theology one's own theological thought can be purified of any experience. A particular social experience underlies Karl Barth's 'epistemological break' with both liberal and orthodox theology: that of the catastrophe of 1914. The collapse of Christian middle-class society, the defeat of the workers' movement and the disappointing course of the 1917 Russian revolution form the historical background to Barth's discovery that the kingdom of God does not arise from the dialectic of history but is an absolutely new element which breaks into history from above. The sole subject of this messianic movement is God himself made incarnate in Christ. This movement *extra nos pro nobis* – for us but outside us – takes place in the event of reconciliation. The liberating reconciliation which forms the centre of Barth's theological thought is an event which has happened once for all in the crucifixion and resurrection of Jesus Christ, and it is the liberating joyful science of this already completed reconciliation that gives people the freedom to be fully active fellow workers in the vineyard of the Lord. In Barth the reconciliation which has already happened – outside us – is the basis of our calling to participate in God's salvation for the world.

In Latin American liberation theology, Barth's powerful stress on the 'already' of the event which has already been fulfilled in Christ gives the impression that the 'not yet' of the unredeemed world, expressed in the inconceivable suffering of the poor, is not really being taken seriously. For Sobrino, L.Boff and others, the poor in their struggle for liberation are fellow subjects in the messianic movement. They form the people of God, which shares in God's history of salvation. The *extra nos* of Christ's work of reconciliation in Barth's Reformation theology is difficult for Latin American theologians to take.

Doubtless traditional differences between the Reformation and Rome play their part here. It is perhaps no coincidence that a Protestant theologian like Míguez Bonino (Argentina) is more restrained than most of his colleagues in a positive assessment of popular religon. Basically, however, the distinction between Barth and liberation theology is connected with the difference in situations: Barth is doing theology at the time of the great catastrophes of the two world wars; the dominant experience of Gutiérrez and his followers is that of the irruption of the poor.

This statement must not be understood in deterministic terms. The recognition of the contextual character of all theological thought has nothing to do with historical determinism. The difference in context is insufficient explanation of the theological conflicts. Our position is that a conversation between Barthian theology and liberation theology can only be meaningful to both sides and contribute to a better understanding of the one universal gospel if the difference in context is carefully assessed.

(d) Those who are absent

The meetings of EATWOT have been very important for the development of Latin American theology.

The methodological perspectives surrounding the notion of theology as the 'second step' were developed in opposition to the initial disapproval and criticism of representatives of other continents, and can no longer be left out of present-day discussions within EATWOT. These insights have also found a place outside the direct context of the Third World. For example, Helmut Gollwitzer has incorporated the method of liberation theology into his farewell lectures *Befreiung zur Solidarität*; feminist theologians from the United States and Europe have used them to advantage, and in his book *De Sodome à l'Exode, Jalons pour une théologie de la libération gaie*, Guy Menard uses the work of Juan Luis Segundo (Uruguay) as a source for his own method of writing a theology of the gay movement.

However, in addition to establishing the legitimate and vital significance of the methodological and hermeneutical starting points of liberation theology, from the beginning there was

criticism within EATWOT of the – closely connected! – use of
Marxist analysis as a tool. Already at the meeting between Latin
American and North American theologians in Detroit in 1975
– a very important conference preceding the establishment of
EATWOT, which was held, after some difficulty, thanks to the
visionary view of the Chilean priest Sergio Torres – it seemed that
liberation did not mean the same thing to feminist, black and Latin
American theologians. Even at that stage the Latin Americans
present had to cope with the criticism that their Marxist class
analysis did not do justice to the distinctive underivable dynamics
of racism and sexism. At the first meeting of EATWOT in
Dar-es-Salaam some participants had difficulties with the Final
Declaration because it was strongly dominated by the Latin
American version of Marxist analysis. The criticism was repeated
at the African conference of EATWOT in Accra, Ghana, in 1977
and the Asian conference in Wennapuwa, Sri Lanka, in 1979 that
the Latin American participants put too much stress on political
and economic oppression and took too little notice of the
marginalization of cultures and religions. James Cone, who made
his presence felt at this conference, continued to express his
dissatisfaction that the black populations and black culture were
as absent from the Latin American theology of liberation as they
were from North American white theology – and that when there
were more black people living in Brazil alone than in the whole
of the United States.

At the time of the preparations for the Latin American Conference of EATWOT in São Paulo in 1980, a serious attempt was
made to cope with this criticism. In order to discuss as fully as
possible the specific forms of oppression to which liberation
theology so far had paid too little attention, three preliminary
meetings were held: of indigenous groups, women and blacks
respectively; unfortunately we can only mention the results briefly
here. The gathering of Latin American women investigated the
way in which the Macho ideology of male superiority, supported
by the patriarchal structure of the institutional church, establishes
and consolidates the capitalist system and in fact represents a
twofold oppression of the *mujer popular*, the great majority of
'ordinary' women'. Although many women are actively involved
in the Christian basic community movement, this has so far not
had enough power to organize and thematize the women's struggle

(a contributory factor is that women have internalized the subjection and passivity enjoined on them by the church's tradition); liberation theology is now faced with the challenge of reformulating its theological categories and reading the Bible from the standpoint of women.

The deliberations of the indigenous (Indian) groups concentrated on the question how the harsh struggle for the right to land and for the preservation of their own culture and identity could be fitted in, both practically and theoretically, to the broad perspective of class struggle and class analysis.

Among the representatives of the black populations of Brazil, Costa Rica and the Caribbean the question arose as to what the liberation envisaged by Latin American theologians meant for their culture and identity; they pointed out how the *branqueamento*, the ideal of the white skin, signifies a permanent crisis for black self-consciousness because of its omnipresence. Alongside this it must be observed that, sadly enough, there was no investigation in São Paulo of the success of Afro-American cults like Umbanda in Brazil; was this passed over in silence because it did not fit into the way in which liberation theology approaches popular religion, which it regards as essentially Christian?

How were the experiences of black indigenous groups and women dealt with in São Paulo? In fact there was a search for theoretical terms of reference within which the fundamental analysis of class oppositions was made deeper, supplemented and corrected by specific analyses of other forms of domination, dependence and liberation. The only question – and it is not a rhetorical question, but a question to which the answer must remain open for the moment – was whether Marxist class theory, in whatever form, is the appropriate instrument for getting to grips with types of racism, sexism and the marginalization of cultures and religions. Within EATWOT it was above all the Asian participants who had their doubts about this. For some of them, Latin American liberation theology, however important its methodological insights may be for Asia and the Third World, is still Western through and through!

This conception certainly does not do justice to the work of Gustavo Gutiérrez and his followers. However, we can begin to understand it to some degree when we see it against the background of the reality of Asia with its enormous variety of religions and cultures, in which barely two per cent of the population has become Christian. What do notions like 'people's church' and 'church of the poor' mean in such situations? We shall in fact be turning to this question in the last chapter of this book.

7

Asian Theology in the Context of Other Religions

In the East, which is the home of half of humanity, even after years of being opened, Western eyes are still hardly in a position to distinguish well the heights and depths of the rich variety of Asian spirituality. So now, at the end of our journey through two-thirds of the world, we have in fact come to the most difficult part. If Latin American theology looks for a portrait in sharp contrasts and primary colours, to do justice to Asian liberation theology in the making we need to have an extremely refined and sophisticated palette full of secondary colours in which a Rembrandt-like chiaroscuro allows light to come out of darkness in a mysterious way. If that is impossible, as it is here, at best we can try to sketch out a basic outline of what emerges from the publications of Asian theologians in past years.

In order to avoid misunderstandings, we emphatically stress that we are not concerned to provide an empirical description of Christian theology in the context of Asia. Although fortunately there is increasing change, the dominant theology in Asian churches remains that of the earlier colonial rulers, and it is this theology which has meant that in many countries the Christian churches formed small, isolated enclaves in a Buddhist, Hindu or Islamic society. This past still has its effect, even where attempts are made to 'adapt' or 'assimilate' to Asian culture and the Asian situation the proclamation of the gospel introduced by mission. The difficulties which were discussed in Chapter 4 in connection with African theology and the method of adaptation also apply here, and need not be raised again. In line with the subject of this book, we shall limit ourselves to a description of the way in which work continues in Asia on a truly contextual, liberating theology which is concerned with the significance of Christ for 'Asia's Struggle for Full Humanity' – the theme of the Asian EATWOT conference in Wennappuwa, Sri Lanka (1979).

Perhaps the best introduction to liberation theology in Asia is a book which was not meant directly to be that. By that we mean *Christian Art in Asia*, edited by Massao Takenaka, Professor of Christian Social Ethics in Kyoto, Japan, which appeared in 1975. The 120 reproductions which Masao Takenaka has included give not only an impressive picture of the creative capacity of Asian artists but are at the same time an 'acccount of the hope that is in you' (I Peter 3.15). In his introduction Takenaka writes: 'Authentic Christian art contains a confession of Christian faith as a personal response by the artist to a particular situation. It is part of the living testimony to the power of Jesus Christ and emerges from the existential experience of the artist who encounters Jesus Christ and gives expression to this experience in a very personal and unique way.'

Masao Takenaka then himself draws the parallel with the search for a living contextual theology which, as is expressed in the consultation *Theology in Action* (Manila 1972), 'begins with the experience of the real struggle, suffering and joys of specific communities'. In fact the works of art presented by Takenaka give an extremely evocative picture of the 'Asian sense' which according to Aloysius Pieris (Sri Lanka) should permeate a truly Asian Third-World theology. Here two things are particularly striking. The first is that the figure of Christ which emerges from most of the paintings is not an exalted figure but the Son of man who identifies himself with the outcasts, prostitutes, tax collectors and lepers; the biblical stories which are portrayed are predominantly those which reflect the suffering and struggle of the people; thus the Exodus of Kim Chung Sook (Korea) conveys the longing of her people on the way from captivity to liberation, and in Noah and his Time by the great Indonesian painter S.Sudjojono, the bewilderment on the face of Noah reflects the anxiety of the artist over the corruption in his country. In the Sorrow of Christ by K.C.S.Paniker (India), Jesus is the personification of suffering and physical human anguish; when Masao Takenaka paid a visit to the commune of young artists established by Paniker (who was born in 1911) in 1964 in Cholamondal, just outside Madras,

Paniker replied to the question why he painted so many pictures of Christ like this: 'I felt attracted by the anguish of Christ. We talk about joy and peace. We do meditation, we fast strictly. But we have nothing to do with physical anguish. However, in Christ I encounter the man who made his love recognizable by giving his own blood.'

It is notable that K.C.S.Paniker is not a Christian but a Hindu. And here we come to the second element that stands out from Masao Takenaka's book. In fact the title *Christian Art in Asia* is somewhat misleading. Quite apart from the question whether it is possible and desirable to use Christian as an adjective in art or culture, a number of reproductions are of works of art by artists who do not call themselves Christian. This raises the question whether it is possible to encounter Christ without giving up one's own cultural and religious tradition. For a number of Asian theologians this has long ceased to be a question, and is a condition of arriving at a living theology in the Asian context. Takenaka's book is so important for theology because it is a fascinating, living and spontaneous illustration of what contextuality means in Asia. Christ does not emerge as a stranger, from outside, but as the one who was made flesh in the midst of the conflict-ridden, complex Asian reality, where the opposition between oppression and liberation, alienation and authenticity, runs through all religions, including Christianity. The means used by Asian artists to express their experiences tend to be derived from their own local surroundings and traditions, and their enormous variety reflects the great differences in culture and religion on the Asian continent. Better than any verbal evidence, *Christian Art in Asia* makes it clear that a Christian theology which wants to open the gospel of Jesus of Nazareth to Asian hearts cannot by-pass the liberating elements of the non-Christian religions. The book confirms and illustrates what Asian theologians have constantly been stressing in ecumenical discussions: that Christ may not be played off against the religious feelings of Asian people because this religiousness has a liberating as well as an oppressive and an alienating dimension. Aloysius Pieris stresses this in his own provocative way in an article in *Concilium* (153, 1982), when he writes:

Gotama, the Buddha, and Muhammad, the Prophet, are house-hold names in the East, but Jesus the Christ is hardly invoked by the vast majority (over ninety-seven per cent) of our people. Yet, Jesus was no less an Asian than the founders of Buddhism and Islam. Even of the few who believe in him, how many recall that God's Word had chosen to become Asian in wanting to be human? And how is it that the first Asians who heard him on our behalf and gave us the normative interpretations of his divine sonship, made a significant breakthough in the West but failed to penetrate the complex cultural ethos of Asia?

Asia's later disillusion with the 'colonial Christ' no doubt added to this estrangement. But it also revealed that Christ could make sense in our cultures only to the extent that we use the soteriological idiom of 'non-Christian religions'. We infer this from the fact that, when Jesus re-entered the continent of his birth as the white colonizer's tribal god seeking ascendancy in the Asian pantheon, it was often the non-Christian religion that awakened the cultural ego of subdued nations in their collisions with Christian powers, so that after four centuries of colonization, Asia would lose only about two per cent of her population to Christianity.

Thus the impression left behind by *Christian Art in Asia* corresponds with what a theologian like Pieris draws attention to: that contextuality in Asia is characterized by two elements or aspects. The first is the element of liberation, of Christ who identifies himself with the suffering and the struggle of the poor – and this discovery of the (oppressed) people as subject of (salvation) history is a bond between the Asian theologian and the Latin American theologian. The second aspect is that of inculturation, which is concerned with the presence of Christ in the religious ethos of non-Christian cultures – and this element gives Asiatic theology a spirituality of its own which is clearly distinct from that of Latin American and other forms of liberation theology.

Each aspect has a history of its own. The liberation theme doubtless was given an important impulse by the inspiration provided by the work of Gutiérrez and others. Above all in the Philippines, the only country in Asia where the majority (eighty-five per cent) count themselves Christians and which historically and socially has some affinity with Latin American countries, the theme of Christ the liberator who identifies himself with the poor finds an echo. But in South Korean Minjung theology, too, the theme of liberation rings out clearly and impressively.

The other aspect, that of inculturation, looks back on a much longer history, traces of which go back to the nineteenth century, when in India both Christian and Hindu theologians bowed before the mystery of Christ and interpreted it in gnostic terms. In fact this theme crops up wherever there is a reflection of 'the problem of the two stories' (D.Preman Niles), the story which the Bible tells and the story of Asian culture and spirituality.

At the EATWOT conference in Wennappuwa, Aloysius Pieris, Director of the Buddhist-Christian Centre for Research and Dialogue at Tulana (Kelaniya, Sri Lanka), gave an important paper in which he located both aspects, liberation and inculturation, in the polarity of Asia's overwhelming poverty and 'multi-faceted religiosity' and presented this polarity of poverty and religion as the *de facto* context of Asian theology. In this way this Jesuit tried to transcend the dilemma, so barren and restrictive for Asian theology, of the conflict between 'Christ against the religions' who rings out in the theme of liberation where the oppressive function of religion is strongly stressed, and the 'Christ of the religions', who is the starting point for the champions of inculturation. According to Pieris, the Asian face of Christ can only be seen when the Asian church gives up its ties with the ruling powers and plays a full part in the struggle of the poor for true humanity:

> It must be humble enough to be baptized in the Jordan of Asian religiosity and bold enough to be baptized on the cross of Asian poverty. Does not the fear of losing its identity make it lean on Mammon? Does not its refusal to die keep it from living? The theology of power-denomination and instrumentalization must give way to a theology of humility, immersion, and participation.

We get the impression that this notion of Pieris has become a real trend-setter for present-day discussions among Asian theologians. However, the lively controversy which followed his contribution shows not only that he had acutely touched on a sensitive spot, but also that by no means everyone was convinced of the possibility and the need to connect the two elements. It is therefore perhaps a good thing to go rather more closely into these two aspects, beginning with inculturation.

(a) The cosmic Christ, creation and human history

In 1959 the Council of Churches for South East Asia made the following pronouncement:

> The Church must endeavour to discern how Christ is at work in the revolution of contemporary Asia... releasing new creative forces, judging idolatry and false gods, leading people to a decision for or against him, and gathering to himself those who respond in faith to him, in order to send them back into the world as witnesses to his kingship. The Church must not only discern Christ in the changing life, but be there in it, responding to him and making his presence and lordship known.

This view clearly expresses the underlying theological perspective of the work of the Christian Institute for the Study of Religion and Society in Bangalore (India), founded in 1956. The founder and first director of this famous institute was Paul David Devanandan (1901–1962). After his death he was succeeded by his associate director, M.M.Thomas, the lay president of the Central Committee of the World Council of Churches (1968–1975). Both have given a decisive impetus to theological thought in Asia.

When in 1961 M.M.Thomas, who stubbornly continues to call himself a 'lay theologian' (originally he studied chemistry and later social sciences and the sociology of religion), gave an address to the Third Assembly of the World Council in New Delhi, which was challenging for the time, he made it quite clear that his theological concern was with the presence of the cosmic Christ in the revolutionary process in which Asia is involved in the wake of decolonization. According to M.M.Thomas, the ecumenical movement has made three important discoveries in the course of its history. These are: 1. The gospel of Jesus Christ transcends all cultural and political orders, social, ideological or ethical systems, and this means that the church must be in a position to involve itself positively, but critically, in creative renewal movements concerned with humanity and the world without absolutizing them. 2. Christ's redemption and judgment are not simply directed at the individual, but are by nature social and cosmic; in other words they embrace the world of science and technology, culture and society, secular theologies and religions. 3. Christ is at work in the world of today, 'involved in a constantly ongoing dialogue with men and peoples, establishing his royal rule over them through the power of his law and his love'. That means that the church may not protect itself from 'the revolutions of our time', but must discern in them Christ's promise and judgment. It is nonsense to suppose that Christ could only be at work through the church or through Christians. He uses secular and non-Christian powers to serve his ends. The church may be expected to recognize Christ in the aspirations and events of our time.

In 1961 M.M. Thomas was speaking against the background of the Asian revolution, that ferment which developed in the colonial period as a result of the Western impact on traditional Asian cultures. Thomas calls on the churches not to retreat into a ghetto but to participate in the building of a new nation. Come what may, Christ is Lord of history; therefore he cannot but be at work in the Asian revolution, which moreover bears within itself the promise of a fuller and richer development of man and society.

Nowhere does M.M.Thomas identify particular historical movements with the work of Christ. Nor does he do this with the Asian revolution. Of course he can speak of 'the struggle for human values as a preparation for the gospel'. In any process of change in history, people are faced with the choice between following the true Messiah and lining up behind the Antichrist. As history progresses, both heaven and hell become a constantly tangible reality, and the sharpness of the conflict between the two increases.

The strong stress which Thomas puts on the effective presence of the cosmic Christ (cf. Col.1; Eph.1) in the always ambivalent process of human history implies the need to investigate its spiritual and material foundations with every possible means. Thus in *The Christian Response to the Asian Revolution* (1966) he gives an accurate description of the different factors and elements which are involved in the Asian ferment of the search for a new society. But Thomas goes even further. In *The Acknowledged Christ of the Indian Renaissance* – the epilogue to which, 'Criteria of an Indian Christian Theology', provoked a good deal of discussion – he investigates the rise of Indian nationalism in the nineteenth century and at the beginning of the twentieth in order to see what significance Christ and Christian belief had for some of the most important spiritual leaders of the Indian renaissance, especially of neo-Hinduism. This interest in figures like Swami Vivekananda, Sri Radhakrishnan and Mahatma Gandhi was nurtured by his belief in the influence of God's kingdom on political, social and spiritual movements, however fragmentary and broken.

In our view the significance of M.M.Thomas for the development of a contextual way of doing theology in South East Asia lies in his stress on the task of the church and theology to recognize Christ's presence in specific historical events. D.Preman Niles, the secretary of the Council of Churches for South East Asia, has rightly observed that Thomas does not approach other religions in terms of their religious character but in terms of their potential for building a human society. Here M.M. (as he is called, for short, by his friends) puts up a dam against abstract, docetic speculations on the relationship of Christ to other religions. Here much of what is summed up under the term theology of religions slips through the cracks, because the specific historical and social context in which religious experiences and phenomena are manifested is not taken into account. The idea of Christ as the fulfilment of the striving for redemption present in all religions (1930 Lambeth Conference, Vatican II) proves to be no more than a suspicious theological abstraction; Thomas also rejects the idea of Christ as a cosmic principle, which is so misleading in the Indian context.

M.M.'s stress on the presence of Christ in the dynamics of history, and his reluctance to see the cosmic Christ in ontological terms as the ground of being which transcends all history, is connected with his theoretically positive evaluation of the process of secularization which came about as a result of the Western impact on Asia and, as far as India is concerned, is not incongruous with certain tendencies towards renewal within Hindu religion and culture. Thomas does not want any lapse into the cosmic monism of the old Eastern civilizations. History as a dynamic process, personal freedom, democracy – these conceptions and values introduced by a Western Christian culture and trampled underfoot by the colonial and imperialistic domination of the same civilization, in themselves represent a step on the way to increasing maturity and adulthood (though at the same time it is true that the more human freedom and human possibilities increase, the more the chance of failure and the deeper the fall). If for M.M.Thomas living theology in Asia is contextual theology, Christ's presence, in whatever situation, must be discerned and explained in the light of Jesus of Nazareth: that is to say, in the light of Christ, incarnate in another situation. For Thomas the story of the Jewish Messiah remains normative.

Other theologians in Asia have much more difficulty than Thomas over the way in which this normativeness is usually expressed. In an essay with the evocative title 'From Israel to Asia: A Theological Leap' (*Mission Trends No.3*, ed. G.H.Anderson and T.F.Stransky), Choan-Seng Song attacks the great theological blunder which began with those theologians who confined God's redemption to the history of the people of Israel and the Christian church and thus institutionalized it and encapsulated it. According to this theologian from Taiwan, Israel was not intended to be the people which mediates God's redeeming love but to be a symbol of the way in which God also deals redemptively with other peoples. Thus the biblical narrative is a paradigm of God's saving love, which is embodied directly and completely in Jesus Christ.

In the fascinating novel *Silence*, by the Japanese writer Shusaku Endo, we are told how foreign missionaries in the seventeenth century were mercilessly persecuted in their attempts to Christianize Japan: at the end of the book there is a conversation between the disillusioned Portuguese priest Rodrigues, who has become an apostate, and Inoue, the lord of Chikugo. Inoue says: 'I have told you that this land of Japan is not suitable for the proclamation of Christian faith. That faith cannot take root here.' For Inoue, the struggle against Christianity is above all a struggle between two conflicting cultures. In his book *Third-Eye Theology* Choan-Seng Song uses Inoue's remark to illustrate his view that the proclamation of God's liberating love must create obedience not outside, but within the spirituality of a particular culture. He is very well aware that this inculturation goes further than adaptation to a fixed church doctrine and other cultural patterns. Song is in fact also in search of a new theological view of creation which finds room for God's redemptive action in other cultures.

In this respect he has met with a welcome from others who, like himself, have found it difficult to do anything with current salvation-historical thought in Western theology. However, Preman Niles regrets that in Song's work the biblical narrative is still too much the norm by which other cultures and histories are measured; in that case the salvation history told through scripture contains in a concentrated form what is present to a lesser degree elsewhere. According to Preman Niles, above all on the basis of what Deutero-Isaiah says about God as the creator who is able to make a completely new beginning in history, it is possible to understand theologically both the elements of discontinuity in the history of the church and the radical irruption of the poor in history. One gets the impression that Preman Niles is in fact looking for an Asian setting of the old hymn *Veni Creator Spiritus*, Come, Creator Spirit.

It is not surprising that much of what Asian theologians write does not rise above the level of a programmatic approach. These beginnings are present in a variety of ways. Thus the Indian theologian Stanley Samartha, for years a valued staff member of the World Council of Churches, in his study *The Hindu Response to the Unbound Christ*, is concerned to lay the foundations of a christology which takes seriously Indian culture and its view of life. Here Samartha uses a central concept from Vedanta philosophy, *advaita*, the unity and completeness of all life, in which nature, man and God are taken up in an everlasting process which has its beginning, continuation and end in *Brahman*. He is aware of the dangers which threaten such an enterprise. Thus he accuses Raymond Panikkar of identifying Christ with Brahman and throwing overboard the historicity of Jesus Christ in his book *The Unknown Christ of Hinduism*. As a result of this, Christ becomes a cosmic ground of meaning and history is volatilized. But Samartha is also opposed to the stress which Western theologians put on history. He looks for a meeting of nature and history, of the historical and the cosmic Christ.

The paper on 'Theological Priorities in India Today' which Samuel Rayan, a priest and theologian as sensitive as he is radical, gave in the name of a number of Indian theologians at the intercontinental EATWOT conference in New Delhi in 1981, is very interesting. It seeks to associate inculturation with the *mukti* – liberation from all that shackles – of the poor and oppressed.

The paper consists of two parts. The first discusses the Indian context, characterized by overwhelming poverty, in which the new middle class – along with industrial magnates, landowners and professional politicians – have a monopoly of political and economic power. One striking feature, certainly compared with the insights of M.M.Thomas, is its positive view of the revival of tribal and ethnic traditions: tribal societies have a means of production which furthers the holistic development of people in society, whereas in capitalism people are used for gain. Harsh criticism of religion is also evident in the paper: generally speaking, religions in India, including the Christian religion, have functioned as bastions safeguarding the power, privileges and exploitation practised by the ruling caste and class. However, the authors of the piece do not reject religion as a result. At the same time, liberating elements are also present in the religious experiences of India.

In the second part of the paper, which discusses theology, belief in Christ is described as a way of seeing with three elements: memory, hope and involvement. Thus theology is the interpretation of things that are seen – of blind people gaining their sight, lame walking again, dead coming to life and poor hearing the news which brings good hope. The authors want to connect this Christian spirituality with the different religious experiences which have emerged in India over the course of history – the cosmic, the gnostic (in which Brahman and Atman coincide as the ultimate reality) and the all-embracing experience of reality (the way of Buddha). These three experiences must be seen as a living unity and interpreted in such a way as to bring out their liberating dimension, robbed of all misuse and manipulation.

It is not clear from the paper precisely how the authors envisage the relationship between the 'Christ-event' and the threefold Indian experience. This lack of clarity is characteristic of the difficulties of solving 'the problem of the two stories'. It is not difficult to put a number of critical questions to Rayan, Samartha, Niles or Song which revolve round the relationship between biblical witness and religious experience. What is the significance of the fact that the name of God may not be spoken in Israel? What does it mean that the first Christians were persecuted as atheists under Roman rule? What of Sobrino's insight that the abandonment of Jesus on the cross is the end of all natural religion? What is the theological significance of the fact that Jesus Messiah was a Jew? Anton G.Honig asks: 'Does not theology constantly go off the rails when we detach the Lordship of Christ and his work in history, including religions, cultures and societies outside Israel, from what he is: the Messiah of Israel?' (*In de Waagschaal*, 1983, no.10).

All these questions can and must be raised. However, in fact they return to us like boomerangs. The 'unbinding' of Christ (to use Samartha's term) from the context of Tenach (the 'Old Testament') is closely connected with the development of dogma as, to use Harnack's terms, a product of the Hellenistic spirit on the soil of the gospel. Moreover, it is very much part of the fact that Christians began to understand themselves as a *tertium genus*, a third race over against Gentiles (*goyim*) and Jews! The disastrous consequences of this whole development are described in detail in 'Theology after Auschwitz'. But Auschwitz is not in Asia. So it does not seem obvious that one should criticize Asian theologians for what is above all a Western problem.

(*b*) Minjung theology

One of the most impressive documents to come out of Asian theology so far is from South Korea, the Asian country which is second only to the Philippines in the size of its Christian population. It is a book called *Minjung Theology. People as the Subjects of History*. The large number of printing errors in the original edition of the book, produced in Singapore, indicates the difficult circumstances in which it was published. The various texts in the book derive from a theological conference of the National Council of Churches in Korea, which was held in Seoul in 1979. Between the time of the conference and the publication of the book in Singapore in 1981, as Preman Niles explains in his Introduction, in the chaotic aftermath of the murder of President Park Chung Hee a number of authors were put in prison, while others had to go underground, and almost all lost their jobs. If we take into account the enormous difficulties accompanying the translation of the texts into English, it is clear how much persistence it took to make Minjung theology known outside Korea.

Minjung literally means 'mass of the people', but it is not easy to convey all the meanings and nuances of the word. The difficulty of defining the term accurately is connected with the fact that 'minjung' is not an object but a living, dynamic reality. The mass, the poor, popular culture, God's people, nation – all these connotations are there. David Kwang-sun Suh says of it:

> The minjung is present where there is talk of social and cultural alienation, economic exploitation and political oppression. So a woman is minjung when she is dominated by her husband, her family or social and cultural structures and factors. An ethnic group is minjung when it is discriminated against politically and economically by another group. A race is minjung when it is dominated by the power of another race, as is the case in the colonial situation. When intellectuals are oppressed because they use their creative and critical capacities against rulers on behalf of the oppressed, they belong to the minjung. Workers and peasants are minjung when they are exploited, when their needs and desires are ignored, and they are crushed by the ruling powers.

The same David Kwang-sun Suh tells how minjung theology arose in the struggle for human rights in the 1970s. It represents theological reflection on the political experiences of workers, students, peasants, writers and theologians in the fight against the harsh dictatorship. It is the work of Christians who are compelled to give an account of their convictions in interrogation centres, prison cells and in the dock before the war council. No wonder that the letters which Dietrich Bonhoeffer wrote from the Berlin prison of Tegel were a special source of inspiration in the development of a 'political hermeneutic of the gospel'.

However, the roots of the Korean Minjung theology go further back than the 1970s. According to Kwang-sun Suh, Korean Protestantism since 1884 has always been aware of the political dimension of the gospel, and that in fact becomes clear from the contribution by Choo Chai Yonh. This church historian stresses the part played by Korean Christians in the struggle for national independence against Japanese domination: 'From the beginning Korean Christianity took shape amidst an oppressed people, and Korean Christians played a leading role in the realization of a national awareness of independence. Korean Christianity never stood aloof from people in their suffering.'

Again according to David Kwang-sun Suh, it was fortunate that in their translation of the Bible the missionaries did not use the Chinese signs which were fashionable among the educated but the language of the ordinary people, the minjung. Reading the Bible in the vernacular meant that the biblical stories came to life in the historical experiences of the oppressed Korean people. It is not surprising, Kwang-sun Suh observes, that the Old Testament and in particular the books of Exodus and Daniel were hated by the Japanese authorities, and later were banned in the church.

The term *han* is an important part of minjung theology. It is even harder to explain this term than the term minjung. Suh Nam Dong calls *han* the most important element in the political and social biography of the minjung. Etymologically speaking, it is a psychological term which expresses the feelings of someone who is oppressed by himself or others. This feeling of *han* is a collective feeling in the collective social biography of the oppressed minjung of Korea. But *han* expresses not only hopelessness; at the same time it is the expression of a positive element, holding fast to the life which emerges from the accumulation of the experience of suffering and provides energy for revolution or rebellion.

For Suh, the popular poet Kim Chi-ha, who was born in 1941, is the embodiment of the subversive power of *han*. For Kim Chi-ha – many times imprisoned, and author of the world-famous 'Declaration of Conscience' and the satire 'The Gold-Crowned Jesus' (performed in the winter of 1976/77 in Japan as a Brechtian Threepenny Opera), the good news of liberation is the content and substance of the gospel, in which 'the unification of God and revolution' transcends any possible social revolution.

Minjung theology does not seek to be Christian theology in the narrow sense of the word. Kim Yong Bock thinks that it is necessary for the messianic political movement in a Korean context 'to rediscover the messianic popular traditions which are inherent in Maitreya messianic Buddhism and the Donghak religion by an investigation of the available literature and by dialogue with Buddhist and Donghak leaders who have the same involvement as we do'.

So although in Minjung theology the stress is on liberation, the element of inculturation is not absent. If at the end of the previous section we could detect in the piece by Samuel Rayan and other Indian theologians that the quest for inculturation goes with a choice for the poor, the opposite is also the case. Neither element can develop in the Asian context without the other.

However, one important problem remains: the question of the real subject of Asian liberation theology. At the conference in Wennappuwa this is what was said in the Final Statement:

> To be truly liberating, this theology must arise from the Asian poor with a liberated consciousness. It is articulated and expressed by the oppressed community using the technical skills of biblical scholars, social scientists, psychologists, anthropologists, and others. It can be expressed in many ways, in art forms, drama, literature, folk stories and native wisdom, as well as in doctrinal-pastoral statements.
>
> Most participants asserted that every theology is conditioned by the class position and class consciousness of the theologian. Hence a truly liberating theology must ultimately be the work of the Asian poor, who are struggling for full humanity. It is they who must reflect on and say what their faith-life experience in the struggle for liberation is. This does not exclude the so-called specialists in theology. With their knowledge they can complement the theologizing of the grassroots people. But their theologizing becomes authentic only when it is rooted in the history and struggle of the poor and the oppressed.

This text is the result of a compromise after a vigorous discussion. In particular the Philippine delegation through their spokesman Carlos Abesamis wanted to go further, convinced that any Third World theology can only arise out of basic communities. Moreover, because of bad experiences with inculturation in their own country, they had difficulties with religion as a second pole in Asian contextual theology.

Although discussion has gone further since Wennappuwa in 1979 and perhaps people have come closer together, the tension between the two poles of poverty and religion has not been wholly resolved. In a continent with so many different political-economic and religious-cultural situations, that hardly seems to be possible.

(c) Towards an ecumenical theology

Over the past ten years Latin American liberation theology has made a great impression in both the Third World and in Europe — and rightly so! It is risky to venture predictions for the future, but it would not surprise us if in coming years interest shifts to

Asian theology. The insights and questions about the importance of non-Christian religions and cultures which are beginning to develop in Asian basic communities and study centres and which are given a favourable dissemination by figures like Samuel Rayan and Aloysius Pieris are so far-reaching that we have still hardly become aware of their implications. What is the significance of Pieris' pronouncement in Wennappuwa (1979) that Asia will always remain a non-Christian continent and that theology in Asia 'is the Christian apocalypse of non-Christian experiences of revelation'? Does this comment mean the end of all Christian theology, or is it the beginning of a new view of the meaning of ecumenicity? Whatever one may think, it is clear that the link between liberation and acculturation in Asia has caused an electrical spark which has set the traditional house of ecumenical discussion on fire.

Of course in recent times this house has also shown plenty of signs of wear – one thinks of all the complaints about the crisis in the ecumenical movement – and it is urgently in need of renovation. It is not inconceivable that the means for this will have to come above all from the continent of 'overwhelming poverty'.

That is not too surprising. In the past, too, Asians have fulfilled important functions in the ecumenical movement. Anyone who thinks back to the Church and Society conference in Geneva in 1966, which proved so decisive for the course of the World Council of Churches, will doubtless remember the decisive contributions by the Indian economist Samuel Parmar and his fellow-countryman M.M.Thomas.

In 1978 the latter made a collection of addresses delivered at ecumenical meetings between 1947 and 1975. He gave the collection the title *Towards a Theology of Contemporary Ecumenism*. The word 'towards' indicates that M.M.Thomas sees his lectures as the ingredients of an ecumenical theology which he still has to produce. As yet there is no truly ecumenical theology, and Thomas will doubtless be troubled that the prospect for it has not improved in recent years. That is *not* because an unstoppable theological emancipation movement has come into being among women, Christians in the Third World and minority groups. It is *certainly* because the ecumenical movement has not been able sufficiently to perform adequately its function as a 'structure of appeal' (L.A. Hoedemaker). In the Faith and Order division, the method of academic theology rejected by EATWOT is still largely predominant. Although EATWOT and Faith and Order both seek to do ecumenical thology, there is a world of difference between them in style and method. We cannot escape the impression that both organizations are theologically miles apart, and that is sad. It seems to suggest that ecumenical theology and contextual theology are mutually exclusive. Which they are not.

Against this background, on the last pages of this book I want to devote some attention to *Towards a Theology of Contemporary Ecumenism*. I am well aware that as a result, in this chapter M.M.Thomas will be too much in the limelight, at the expense of others who undeservedly remain anonymous.

If anyone in his life and work has shown that ecumenical élan and local involvement, particularity and universality, belong together and presuppose each other, it is M.M.Thomas. The different functions that he has performed in the ecumenical movement have never prevented him from being deeply involved in what is happening in his own land and in his own church, the Mar Thoma church; it is typical of him that over recent years he has constantly been at work on a series of biblical commentaries, written as simply as possible in the language of his region, Malayalam. Theologically we can see the connection between particularity and universality in his work when we note the place occupied by the terms salvation, liberation and redemption. If I am right, three levels can be distinguished in his approach to messianic salvation: an eschatological, a cultural-anthropological and a socio-political level.

1. *The socio-political level.* In his speech to the fifth assembly of the World Council of Churches in Nairobi in 1975, Thomas said: 'the rediscovery of the Christ of the poor and oppressed is the basis of the solidarity and identification of the Church with those struggling for liberation.' It is the task of the church and of individual Christians to share in the struggle for social justice. He described this justice in an address in Singapore in 1973 as 'the transformation of existing structures of state, economic order and society so that the poor and oppressed may become full participants in the total life of society'. The church, which is there for all, is only the church when it identifies itself with the poor

(this notion implies sharp criticism of his own Mar Thoma church, to which Thomas nevertheless feels a deep loyalty).

2. *The cultural-anthropological level.* In fact the social and political liberation of oppressed classes, races, sexes and peoples is part of a process which embraces the history of mankind as a whole. Thomas sees history as a process in which human beings develop increasingly towards adulthood. In modern history, this process of liberation has three important long-term aspects: (*a*) the ongoing revolution of science and technology, which frees human beings from being tied to nature; (*b*) the new self-awareness of peoples who hitherto have been oppressed and have not made a mark in history; (*c*) the world-wide process of secularization, which represents a liberation from static social structures and from permanent norms established for all times. It is striking how Thomas keeps returning to these three features, albeit in different words. In Uppsala 1968 he affirmed that the difference between salvation history and secular history has done theology no good. The ecumenical movement only makes sense if it becomes the foundation of a new humanism in which Christ is recognized as the new man whose kingdom influences the wide-ranging process of change in our time.

However, the Antichrist is also present in history. What implies a promise of a richer human existence can be a great threat: science and technology can lead to self-annihilation; liberation from oppression can be perverted into self-assertion; secularization can become secularism. The church is the body which must see that the human goals of liberation are not corrupted. The church has to learn the intrinsic ambivalence of human action. As the community of sinners who live by forgiveness, it knows that all human liberation stands in the shadow of God's judgment and redemption, and in this sense it is God's instrument of permanent revolution. M.M.Thomas ends his speech 'Jesus Christ Frees and Unites' in Nairobi 1975 by saying, 'Jesus, God incarnate, crucified by all that was best in church, community and state of his time, reveals the idolatrous spirit of human bondage which works in every unity we realize; the risen Jesus is the guarantee of a total liberation from sin and death for a new humanity that awaits us in the end and which already works in history as the instrument of the permanent liberation.'

3. *The eschatological level.* Just as the cultural and anthropo-

logical level includes the social and political level, so the eschatological level includes both. Eschatological freedom is not something on which Christians can fall back in any political and
social choice. On the contrary, it is the antidote to statistical
interpretations of Christian doctrinal positions and Christian
morality. The churches stand under God's judgment because of
their inability to be a foretaste of the new humanity in Christ and
because of their lack of solidarity with those who are struggling
for liberation. Christ as the new man remains the criterion in the
struggle for a more humane society. M.M.Thomas believes in a
creative tension between eschatology and history. There is no
continuity between the humanity achieved by men and women in
history and the eschatological humanity of Jesus Christ. Therefore
history stands under the judgment of the new man, who still
remains God's promise and offer in Christ Jesus.

There is an unmistakable affinity between the theological
insights of M.M.Thomas and those of the Latin American theologians. The three levels of significance that we thought we could
distinguish in M.M.Thomas are also present in Gustavo Gutiérrez.
In his *Theology of Liberation* Gutiérrez distinguishes 1. political
liberation; 2. human liberation in the course of history; 3.
liberation from sin, and entering into communion with God. With
him, too, the three levels can be distiguished but not separated.
The difference is, however, that in Latin American theology there
is a much more critical attitude towards such 'Western' values as
maturity, freedom and democracy, while on the other hand, in
contrast to Thomas, there is talk of a factor of continuity between
history and eschatology, namely the struggle and the suffering of
the poor.

However, both in Latin American theology and with
M.M.Thomas the indissoluble connection between the three levels
guarantees a connection between particularity and universality,
situational involvement and ecumenical élan. The Asian tone of
Thomas' thought here can clearly be discerned from the way in
which he discusses the relationship between Christian faith and
other religions as an ecumenical problem. He is strongly opposed
to a privatized conception of the gospel, which for him is a centre
of meaning and sanctification not only for individuals but also
for cultures. In the history of different cultures there is a search
for a total context in which people find fulfilment. Thomas calls

this capacity spirituality. In Bangkok, 1972, he gives the following description of this concept, which is fundamental to Asian theology: 'Human spirituality, one might say, is the way in which man, in the freedom of his self-transcendence, seeks a structure of ultimate meaning and sacredness within which he can fulfil or realize himself in and through his involvement in the bodily, the material and the social realities and relations of his life on earth.'

There is, however, as it were a false spirituality. The important thing is where spirituality is directed: 'Human spirituality undergirds all human strivings for health and sex, for development and justice. The only question is whether it is a true or a false spirituality, that is, whether the structure of ultimate meaning and sacredness to which it is committed is the meaning and sacredness which is truly ultimate, i.e. of God, or simply created by men in their self-centredness and rejection of God, and therefore idolatrous.' The church must look for this true spirituality by participating in movements which aim at the liberation of human life, in such a way that 'in the middle of these streams we bear witness to Jesus Christ as the source, the judge and the liberator of human spirituality'. In Nairobi 1975 he describes this task as 'spirituality for combat' (taking the expression from David Jenkins).

Before we suspect Thomas of calling for too great a change in the church, we must take into account the fact that he stresses that the creation of structures of true spirituality ultimately does not depend on the church but on the Messiah himself who goes before us: 'I have spoken of the choice between God as he has revealed himself in Christ and the idols made by men in the sphere of the structures of meaning and the sacred. By that I do not mean the choice between "Christianity" and "the other religions". In fact the dividing line between God and the idols runs straight through both Christianity and religion.' This last notion underlies Thomas' summons to the Nairobi assembly to be more serious about attempts to discern how Christ is at work in other religions. He argues for a Christ-centred syncretism, a process in which any religion and ideology is critically evaluated and relativized in the light of God's grace in Jesus Christ. This is an inescapable task for a contemporary ecumenical theology.

In August 1981 EATWOT held an international conference in

New Delhi to discuss the results of five years shared work and to set out guidelines for the future. The theme was 'Irruption of the Third World'. Two things are particularly striking in comparison with the first meeting in Dar-es-Salaam. As *The Emergent Gospel*, the book about Dar-es-Salaam, shows, the only contribution from the women present there was that by Beatriz Melano Couch (Argentina), and her contribution was not about the position of women in the Third World but about Latin American Protestantism. At all events, in New Delhi the discontent over the exclusion of women came to the boil – Mercy Amba Oduyoye of Nigeria spoke of an irruption within the irruption – and in the Final Statement the breakthrough by women was said to be an unmistakeable element in the development of Third World theology. A second important difference from Dar-es-Salaam was the concern for non-Christian cultures and religions. According to the Final Statement, people from other religions and beliefs also reveal aspects of God's will and message for our time. There is considerable agreement with what we heard M.M. Thomas say and the New Delhi statement that the basic opposition is not that between Christian faith and atheism or between Christianity and other religions but between the God of life and the false gods who destroy life.

We end this book with a passage from the Final Statement:

We find the Third World a dialectical tension between life and death, manifested in different ways. In Asia, despite the tendency to reconcile and harmonize opposites, this tension between strong affirmation of life and emphatic renunciation of life continues. In the African worldview, the cosmos is seen as a permanent struggle between life and death. In Latin America, physical death of the victims of repression has become a source of life for the Christian community. This dialectical relationship challenges us to deepen the meaning of our faith in the God of life. Third World theology is thus led to a constitutive dimension of our biblical faith: through Jesus' death, God overcame death (II Tim.1.10). God has overcome death in all its forms and shapes. This is the source of our hope that life-giving forces will finally triumph. To believe in this God of life is to believe in love, justice, peace, truth and human fulfilment. It is to denounce causes of the dehumanization of our people and to fight against the systems that shorten and extinguish the lives of so many.

To proclaim a God who does not see the plight of the poor and does not act in their favour is to preach a God of death, a dead God. When the forces of death are free to kill, God's reality is not recognized. When life is ignored or cruelly crushed, false Gods are set up. This is idolatry. In the Third World, the opposite of faith is not atheism but idolatry.

Bibliography

Chapter 1

Walbert Buhlmann, *The Missions on Trial*, Middlegreen, Slough: St Paul and Maryknoll, New York: Orbis Books 1979

Paulo Freire, *Pedagogy of the Oppressed*, Harmondsworth: Penguin Books and New York: Seabury 1972

Eduardo Galeano, *The Open Veins of Latin America. Five Centuries of the Pillage of a Continent*, New York and London: Monthly Review 1973

Walter Rodney, *How Europe Underdeveloped Africa*, Washington, DC: Howard University Press and London: Bogle-L'Ouverture Publications 1978

Chapter 2

Gerald H.Anderson and Thomas F.Stransky, CSP (eds.), *Mission Trends No.3, Third World Theologies*, New York: Paulist Press and Grand Rapids: William B.Eerdmans 1976

Gerald H.Anderson and Thomas F.Stransky, CSP (eds.), *Mission Trends No.4, Liberation Theologies*, New York: Paulist Press and Grand Rapids: William B.Eerdmans 1979

Robert McAfee Brown, *Theology in a New Key: Responding to Liberation Themes*, Philadelphia: Westminster Press 1978

European Theology Challenged by the World-Wide Church, Conference of European Churches, Occasional Paper No.8, Geneva 1976

Alfredo Fierro, *The Militant Gospel. An Analysis of Contemporary Political Theologies*, Maryknoll, New York: Orbis Books and London: SCM Press 1977

Brian Mahan and L.Dale Richesin (eds.), *The Challenge of Liberation Theology, A First World Response*, Maryknoll, New York: Orbis Books 1981

Jon Sobrino, *The True Church and the Poor*, Maryknoll, New York: Orbis Books 1984 and London: SCM Press 1985

Sergio Torres and John Eagleson (eds.), *Theology in the Americas*, Maryknoll, New York: Orbis Books 1976

Sergio Torres and Virginia Fabella, MM (eds.)., *The Emergent Gospel. Theology from the Underside of History*, Papers from the Ecumenical

Dialogue of Third World Theologians, Dar-es-Salaam, August 5-12, 1976, EATWOT 1, Maryknoll, New York:Orbis Books 1978

Chapter 3

(*a*) Racism and slavery

Pierre L. van den Berghe, *Race and Racism. A Comparative Perspective*, New York: Wiley ²1978

David Brion Davis, *The Problem of Slavery in Western Culture*, Ithaca, New York: Cornell University Press 1966

Eugene D.Genovese, *The World the Slaveholders Made*, New York: Pantheon 1969

Eugene D.Genovese, *Roll, Jordan Roll. The World the Slaves Made*, New York: Pantheon 1974

Winthrop D.Jordan, *White over Black: American Attitudes Toward the Negro, 1550-1812*, New York: Norton 1977

Donald G.Mathews, *Religion in the Old South*, Chicago: University of Chicago Press 1977

Léon Poliakov, *The Aryan Myth. History of Racist and Nationalist Ideas in Europe*, New York: New American Library 1980

Barbara Rogers, *Race: No Peace without Justice. Churches Confront the Mounting Racism of the 1980s*, Geneva: WCC 1980

R.Ross (ed.), *Racism and Colonialism*, The Hague 1982

Eric Williams, *Capitalism and Slavery*, New York: Russell 1961 (reissue of 1944 edition)

(*b*) Black theology in the United States

James H.Cone, *Black Theology and Black Power*, New York: Seabury 1969

James H.Cone, *For My People: Black Theology and the Black Church*, Maryknoll, New York: Orbis Books 1984

James H.Cone, *God of the Oppressed*, New York: Seabury 1975

Vincent Harding, *There is a River. The Black Struggle for Freedom in America*, New York: Harcourt, Brace, Jovanovich 1981

William R.Jones, *Is God a White Racist?*, Garden City, New York: Anchor Press 1973

C.Eric Lincoln (ed.), *The Black Experience in Religion*, Garden City, New York: Anchor Press 1974

Albert J.Raboteau, *Slave Religion. The 'Invisible Institution' in the Antebellum South*, New York: Oxford University Press 1978

J.Deotis Roberts, *Liberation and Reconcilation: A Black Theology*, Philadelphia: Westminster Press 1971

Joseph R.Washington, *Black Religion*, Boston: Beacon Press 1964

Gayraud S.Wilmore, *Black Religion and Black Radicalism: An*

Interpretation of the Religious History of Afro-American People, second edition, revised and enlarged, Maryknoll, New York: Orbis Books 1983

Gayraud S.Wilmore and James H.Cone (ed.), *Black Theology; A Documentary History, 1966-1979*, Maryknoll, New York: Orbis Books 1979

(c) Black theology in the South African system of apartheid

Allan Boesak, *Farewell to Innocence*, Maryknoll, New York: Orbis Books 1978

Allan Boesak, *Black and Reformed: Apartheid, Liberation and the Calvinist Tradition*, Maryknoll, New York: Orbis Books and Johannesburg, South Africa: Skotaville 1984

Marjorie Hope and James Young, *The South African Churches in a Revolutionary Situation*, Maryknoll, New York: Orbis Books 1981

Bernard Mahosezwe Magubane, *The Political Economy of Race and Class in South Africa*, New York and London: Monthly Review 1979

Basil Moore (ed.), *Black Theology: The South African Voice*, London: C.Hurst 1974

Desmond B.Tutu, *Hope and Suffering: Sermons and Speeches*, Grand Rapids, Mich.: William B.Eerdmans, Johannesburg, South Africa: Skotaville 1983, and London: Collins 1984

Peter Walshe, *Church versus State in South Africa. The Case of the Christian Institute*, London: C.Hurst and Maryknoll, New York: Orbis Books 1983.

Chapter 4

Kofi Appiah-Kubi and Sergio Torres (eds.), *African Theology En Route*, Papers from the Pan-African Conference of Third World Theologians, December 17-23, 1977, Accra, Ghana, EATWOT II, Maryknoll, New York: Orbis Books 1979

F.Eboussi Boulaga, *Christianity without Fetishes: An African Critique and Recapture of Christianity*, Maryknoll, New York: Orbis Books 1984

Basil Davidson, *Africa in Modern History. The Search for a New Society*, Harmondsworth: Penguin Books 1978

Kwesi A.Dickson, *Theology in Africa*, London: Darton, Longman and Todd, and Maryknoll, New York: Orbis Books 1984

Kwesi A.Dickson and Paul Ellingworth (eds.), *Biblical Revelation and African Beliefs*, Guildford: Lutterworth Press 1969

Edward Fashole-Luké, Richard Gray, Adrian Hastings and Godwin Tasie (eds.), *Christianity in Independent Africa*, London: Rex Collings 1978

Adrian Hastings, *A History of African Christianity 1950-1975*, Cambridge: Cambridge University Press 1979

John S.Mbiti, *African Religions and Philosophy*, London: Heinemann Educational and New York: Doubleday 1969

Gwinyai H.Muzorewa, *The Origins and Development of African Theology*, Maryknoll, New York: Orbis Books 1985

Nathanel I. Ndiokwere, *Prophecy and Revolution. The Role of Prophets in the Independent African Churches and in Biblical Tradition*, London: SPCK 1981

Aylward Shorter, *African Christian Theology. Adaptation or Incarnation?*, London: Geoffrey Chapman and Maryknoll, New York: Orbis Books 1975

Chapter 5

Leonard E.Barrett, *The Rastafarians. The Dreadlocks of Jamaica*, London: Heinemann Educational 1977

Sebastian Clarke, *Jah Music. The Evolution of the Popular Jamaican Song*, London: Heinemann Educational 1980

Stephen Davis and Peter Simon, *Reggae International*, London: Thames and Hudson 1983

Noel Leo Erskine, *Decolonizing Theology. A Caribbean Perspective*, Maryknoll, New York: Orbis Books 1981

Idris Hamid (ed.), *Troubling of the Waters*, San Fernando, Trinidad 1973

Idris Hamid (ed.), *Out of the Depths*, San Fernando, Trinidad 1977

Amy Jacques Garvey, *The Philosophy and Opinions of Marcus Garvey*, New York: F.Cass Company 1974

Joseph Owens, *Dread: The Rastafarians of Jamaica*, London: Heinemann Educational 1976

Walter Rodney, *The Groundings with my Brothers*, London:Bogle L'Ouverture and New York: Panther House 1971

Chapter 6

Leonardo Boff, *Jesus Christ Liberator: A Critical Christology for Our Time*, Maryknoll, New York: Orbis Books and London: SPCK 1978

Leonardo Boff and Clodovis Boff, *Salvation and Liberation*, Maryknoll, New York: Orbis Books and Melbourne: Dove Books 1984

José Míguez Bonino, *Doing Theology in a Revolutionary Situation*, Philadelphia: Fortress Press and London SPCK 1975

James R.Brockman, *The Word Remains: A Life of Oscar Romero*, Maryknoll, New York: Orbis Books and London: Sheed and Ward 1982

Edward L.Cleary, *Crisis and Change: The Church in Latin America*, Maryknoll, New York: Orbis Books 1985

Enrique Dussel, *A History of the Church in Latin America*, Grand Rapids: William B.Eerdmans 1982

John Eagleson and Philip Scharper (eds.), *Puebla and Beyond: Documentation and Commentary*, Maryknoll, New York: Orbis Books 1979

Rosino Gibellini (ed.), *Frontiers of Theology in Latin America*, Maryknoll, New York: Orbis Books and London: SCM Press 1979

Gustavo Gutiérrez, *Theology of Liberation*, Maryknoll, New York: Orbis Books and London: SCM Press 1974

Gustavo Gutiérrez, *We Drink from our Own Wells: The Spiritual Journey of a People*, Maryknoll, New York: Orbis Books, London: SCM Press and Melbourne: Dove 1984

Penny Lernoux, *Cry of the People. The Struggle for Human Rights in Latin America – The Catholic Church in Conflict with US Policy*, Harmondsworth: Penguin Books 1982

Juan Luis Segundo, *The Liberation of Theology*, Maryknoll, New York: Orbis Books and Dublin: Gill and Macmillan 1976

Jon Sobrino, *Christology at the Crossroads: A Latin American Approach*, Maryknoll, New York: Orbis Books and London: SCM Press 1978

Sergio Torres and John Eagleson (eds.), *The Challenge of Basic Christian Communities*. Papers from the International Ecumenical Congress of Theology, February 20 – March 2, 1980, São Paulo, Brazil, EATWOT IV, Maryknoll, New York: Orbis Books 1981

Chapter 7

Tissa Balasuriya, *Planetary Theology*, Maryknoll, New York: Orbis Books and London: SCM Press 1984

Commission on Theological Concerns of the Christian Conference of Asia (eds.), *Minjung Theology: People as the Subjects of History*, revised edition, Maryknoll, New York: Orbis Books, London: Zed Press and Singapore: Christian Conference of Asia 1983

D.J.Elwood (ed.), *What Asian Christians are Thinking*, Quezon City: New Day Publishers 1976

John England (ed.), *Living Theology in Asia*, London: SCM Press and Maryknoll, New York: Orbis Books 1982

Virginia Fabella (ed.), *Asia's Struggle for Full Humanity: Towards a Relevant Theology*. Papers from the Asian Theological Conference, January 7-20, 1979, Wennapuwa, Sri Lanka, EATWOT III, Maryknoll, New York: Orbis Books 1980

Virginia Fabella, MM, and Sergio Torres (ed.), *Irruption of the Third World: Challenge to Theology*. Papers from the Fifth International Conference of the Ecumenical Association of Third World Theologians, August 17-29, 1981, New Delhi, India, EATWOT V, Maryknoll, New York: Orbis Books 1983

Virginia Fabella, MM, and Sergio Torres (ed.), *Doing Theology in a Divided World*. Papers from the Sixth International Conference of the Ecumenical Association of Third World Theologians, January 5-13,

1983, Geneva, Switzerland, EATWOT VI, Maryknoll, New York: Orbis Books 1985

Anton G.Hongi, *Trends in Present Asian Theology*, Exchange, nos.32-33, Leiden 1982 (followed by M.R.Spindler, *The Biblical Factor in Asian Theology*)

Marianne Katopo, *Compassionate and Free*. An Asian Woman's Theology, Maryknoll, New York: Orbis Books 1979

Kosuke Koyama, *Mount Fuji and Mount Sinai*, London: SCM Press 1984 and Maryknoll, New York: Orbis Books 1985

Choan-Seng Song, *Third-Eye Theology*, Maryknoll, New York: Orbis Books and Guildford: Lutterworth Press 1979

Choan-Seng Song, *Tell Us Our Names: Story Theology from an Asian Perspective*, Maryknoll, New York: Orbis Books 1984

Masao Takenaka, *Christian Art in Asia*, Kyoto: Kyo Bun Kwan 1975

M.M.Thomas, *The Acknowledged Christ of the Indian Renaissance*, London: SCM Press 1969

M.M.Thomas, *Towards a Theology of Contemporary Ecumenism*, Madras: Christian Literature Society 1978

Index of Names

J